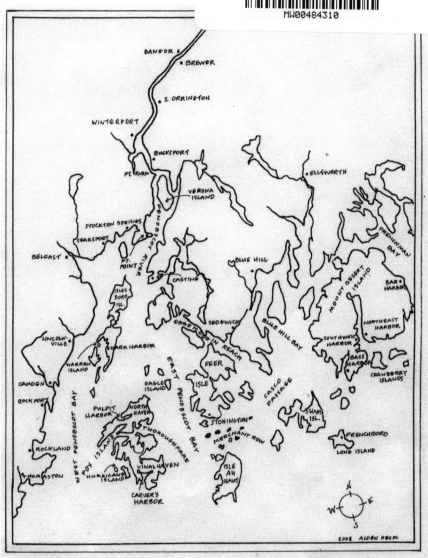

Map of Penobscot Bay. *Courtesy of Alden Heck.*

HISTORIC SHIPWRECKS

of

PENOBSCOT BAY

HARRY GRATWICK

Charleston · London

THE
History
PRESS

Published by The History Press
Charleston, SC 29403
www.historypress.net

Copyright © 2014 by Harry Gratwick
All rights reserved

First published 2014

Manufactured in the United States

ISBN 978.1.62619.091.7

Library of Congress CIP data applied for.

The man who has experienced shipwreck shudders even at a calm sea.
—Ovid

Contents

CONTENTS

Acknowledgements

During the preparation of this book, I received a great deal of support from two people. Jon Johansen is editor of the *Maine Coastal News* and was an invaluable source of information about Penobscot Bay shipwrecks. I am also grateful to Captain John Flint, who kindly shared his notes on the wrecks of HMS *Albany* and SS *Cambridge* with me, as well as his years of research on the British sea captain Henry Mowat.

I would also like to thank the following people for their help on specific shipwrecks: Dick Eichacker, Larkin Post and Jim Quinn at the Marshall Point Lighthouse Museum in Port Clyde; Stephen Puleo, for his help with USS Eagle 56; Betsy Paradis, Special Collections librarian at the Belfast Free Library; Bill Booth at the Maine Historical Society; Kelly Page and Nathan Lipfert at the Maine Maritime Museum; Cipperly Good, Charles Mason and Kevin Johnson at the Penobscot Marine Museum; Dan O'Conor at the Rockland Public Library; and David Hock at the Rockland Historical Society.

On Islesboro, historians Paul Pendleton and Nancy Alexander were gracious with their assistance, and on Isle au Haut, I am indebted to historian Harold van Doren for his images and information on USS *Adams* that was wrecked off that island.

On Vinalhaven, I give my thanks to Stephen Stontheimer, who took me in his boat to photograph the ledges in Penobscot Bay, where many of the wrecks occurred. And as always, I appreciate the assistance and advice I received from Roy Heisler, Ken Reiss, Bill Chilles and Lauretta Chilles at the Vinalhaven Historical Society, as well as Valerie Morton and Linda Whittington at the Vinalhaven Library. Finally, my love and many thanks to my wife, Tita, an invaluable editor and a whole lot more.

Introduction

On a foggy July morning in the early 1950s, I was awakened by the sound of angry voices coming from the water near our cabin on Vinalhaven Island. As the fog slowly lifted, I saw the shape of a forty-foot motorboat perched on Raspberry Rock, half a mile away. Further investigation revealed that the stranded craft was the elegant *JO* from North Haven; it had strayed off course. I rowed out to the scene for a closer look and, during the course of my inspection, took several pictures.

JO was floated off Raspberry Rock on the next tide, so I never did find out the details of the accident; presumably it lost its bearings in the fog. Certainly the captain, seen in the picture, was not about to tell a curious lad what had gone wrong.

You cannot grow up on the rugged Maine coast without becoming aware of the perils of the sea. (As a child, I remember when three young fishermen from Vinalhaven drowned when their dory tipped over.) Of the many hazardous navigation areas on the eastern seaboard, the rocky shores of Maine are among the most treacherous. Although fewer lives are lost in twenty-first-century storms, it is hard to comprehend how difficult it was to maneuver a ship in poor weather before the days of space-age navigation.

While shipping accidents still happen, they were legion in the days before Global Positioning System (GPS) and radar were developed. Penobscot Bay has had its share of disasters. Vinalhaven suffered the loss of six fishing schooners that were attempting to ride out a nasty storm in Matinicus Harbor in October 1841. Farther up the Bay, the town of Castine lost

The North Haven boat *JO* seen stuck on Raspberry Rock off Granite Island, Vinalhaven, circa 1952. *Author's collection.*

fourteen vessels and fifty-one men in the years between 1839 and 1867. And nearby Belfast lost eleven vessels and thirty sailors in the same period. Wayne O'Leary wrote in *Maine Sea Fisheries*, "Altogether, during the half century ending in 1889 at least fifty-nine schooners and ninety-seven fishermen, approximately one vessel and two men each year, were lost from the various towns bordering Penobscot Bay."

There is something mysterious about a shipwreck. What was it that caused the wreck? In many cases, we will never know the whole story and can only speculate. Many, like *JO*, presumably got lost in the fog and subsequently ran on the rocks. There were ships like the schooner *Alice E. Clark* that would appear to have simply strayed off course in clear weather. Others, like *Pentagoet*, disappeared in storms like the Portland Gale, which devastated the Maine coast in 1898, or were consumed by fire, like the circus ship *Royal Tar*. Then there were vessels like *City of Rockland* that, after repeated accidents, were deemed not worthy of repair and were taken out of service and destroyed. Finally, some were "put out to pasture" like *Hesper* and *Luther Little*, which spent their last years rotting in the mud on the banks of the Sheepscot River near the bridge at Wiscasset.

The ships discussed in this book represent a sampling of the many accidents and disasters that have occurred in Penobscot Bay ships over the last three centuries. Of the hundreds of shipwrecks, I have selected a variety of the vessels that have been destroyed since HMS *Albany* ran on the ledges of Penobscot Bay's Northern Triangles in 1782.

Part I
Four Warships from Three Centuries

The warships that are discussed in this part include two that were enemy vessels and two that were American. The sinkings span four of the wars in which the United States was involved, starting with the American Revolution and running through World War II. HMS *Albany* was a British sloop of war that sank in 1782. USS *Adams* was an American sloop that was burned in the middle of the War of 1812. CSS *Georgia* was a Confederate raider made in England that sank following the Civil War. USS *Eagle 56* was a submarine chaser built at the end of World War I that was used throughout World War II. Significantly, it was the last American warship to be sunk by a German submarine, in 1945.

LOST CANNONS: THE WRECK OF HMS *ALBANY*

The Northern Triangles are an extensive series of ledges located at the southern entrance to Penobscot Bay. Even in the twenty-first century, sailors passing through Two Bush Channel need to beware of getting off course for fear of running into a large minefield of rocks, most of which lie just below the ocean's surface at low tide.

Captain John Flint, who lives in Cushing, Maine, has researched a number of Penobscot Bay shipwrecks, including the wreck of HMS *Albany*.

John Flint is a retired sea captain who has researched a number of Penobscot Bay shipwrecks. *Author's collection.*

The Northern Triangles are barely visible at low tide. Little Green Island is seen in background. *Author's collection.*

One day, his friend Richard Spear told him the story of the wreck of *Albany* and where the remains of the ship were located. Flint passed the information along to two local fishermen, who, after trolling the ledges of Northern Triangles, found two cannons lodged in the crevasses of some rocks that were barely visible at low tide.

The fishermen hauled the cannons into their boat, took them home and informed the state archaeological authorities of their discovery. Word came back from the state that they had no right to take the cannons, or any other parts of the ship they had found, and to put everything back. The fishermen dutifully told state authorities that they had done so. Exactly where the cannons lie today, however, remains a mystery.

This is the story of HMS *Albany* and of how the ship ran on the Northern Triangles during a winter storm in the last days of the American Revolution.

Henry Mowat

At the start of the American Revolution, Henry Mowat (1734–1798) was a frustrated British naval officer who had spent nearly twenty years of what would be a forty-three-year career patrolling the North American coast. Mowat, who was probably more familiar with the New England coast than any other British naval officer, first came to North America in 1758 as a twenty-four-year-old. As the years passed, he was promised "improved commands," but for reasons that will be explained, promotions were slow in coming.

Mowat came from good seafaring stock. Some say that one of his ancestors was a survivor of the Spanish Armada who ended up in northern Scotland in 1590. Young Henry grew up on the wind-swept Orkney Islands. His father, Captain Patrick Mowat, commanded a ship on Captain James Cook's first global voyage in the 1760s, and his three brothers were also navy men.

At the conclusion of the French and Indian War in 1763, Mowat was ordered to guard a survey expedition for the official cartographer of King George III. For the next twelve years, Mowat guided royal survey ships along the Atlantic coast from Newfoundland to the Virginias. Most of this time, he was skipper of *Canceaux*. As relations with American colonies worsened in the early 1770s, the *Canceaux* was converted from a three-masted merchant ship into an armed vessel.

Wesleyan Professor James Stone wrote that by the start of the American Revolution, "[Mowat's] many years on the survey of the coast to the

Henry Mowat was a British naval officer who spent twelve years surveying the New England coast and the St. Lawrence River before the American Revolution. *Courtesy of Maine Historical Society/Maine Memory Network.*

eastward of Boston and his knowledge of all the harbors, bays and creeks and shoals resulted in his being the most knowledgeable and experienced naval commander in British North America, bar none."

Following the Battles of Lexington and Concord, rebel forces captured Henry Mowat near Falmouth (present-day Portland) on May 7, 1775. He was released, having given his word of honor to his captors that he would return the next morning. Mowat broke his parole, however, and fled in his ship *Canceaux* to Boston.

British admiral Samuel Graves, commander of the North American Station, had been given an impossible task. At the start of the Revolution, his assignment was to oversee a blockade of the entire American coast with a mere thirty ships. Poor Graves was in over his head and was unable to stop the harassment of British ships that went on in the months and years that followed.

Graves's orders came from First Lord of the Admiralty John Montagu, Earl of Sandwich: "Exert yourself to the utmost towards crushing the daring rebellion." Graves accordingly directed Henry Mowat to "proceed along the coast and lay waste, burn and destroy such seaport towns as are accessible to His Majesty's ships…to make the most vigorous efforts to burn the towns and destroy the shipping." Graves added that it was up to Mowat to go wherever he wanted.

Mowat arrived in Casco Bay on the evening of October 16, 1775, in command of three small warships and proceeded to disobey Admiral Graves's orders. The next morning, he sent a barge to Falmouth with a letter to the town fathers stating that he had orders to fire on the town immediately. Mowat added that he would "deviate from his orders" and give the townspeople two hours to evacuate the next morning. Captain Mowat emphasized that his orders could not be changed and that he was already risking the loss of his commission by giving the town a warning. It turned out to be a decision that would haunt him for the rest of his career.

It took Mowat most of October 17 to get his ships into position, and on the morning of October 18, he then waited an additional half hour before beginning to bombard Falmouth. At 3:00 p.m., he then sent landing parties ashore to set fire to buildings not demolished by gunfire. It is estimated that more than four hundred structures were destroyed, leaving most of the town homeless.

Professor Stone wrote, "Mowat's name would go down in infamy." Nearly 130 years later, Portland journalist C.E. Banks compared Mowat to Nero: "His unparalleled barbarity was exploited abroad and his name finally consigned to that limbo of hopeless condemnation where he will be remembered by future generations as a fiend and not as a man."

There are those who consider Mowat a "war criminal" for ordering the destruction of Falmouth in October 1775. George Washington would later write of his action, "I know not how to detest it." While American revolutionaries saw him as a destroyer, Loyalists considered him the heroic savior of Fort George and the town of Castine. Although Mowat would prove to be the indispensible man in the defense of Castine in 1779, his name would be forever tarnished by the notoriety he received as the destroyer of Falmouth, as well as for having broken his parole.

His name was also not respected as a British naval officer. From the military perspective, he was seen as disobeying Graves's orders by warning the town of his imminent attack. The result was that for the rest of his career, promotions were slow in coming to Mowat, leaving him an embittered man.

Following the destruction of Falmouth, Mowat requested and was given command of HMS *Albany*, which was purchased by the Royal Navy in 1776. In his research into the sinking of *Albany*, Captain John Flint thought that the ship was probably the former American sloop *Howe*. *Albany* was wider and newer than Mowat's decrepit old *Canceaux*. Although far from an ideal vessel, Mowat considered it an improvement over his previous command.

The British purchased American-built sloops like *Albany* in great numbers during the American Revolution, but their shallow drafts and poor accommodations for officers and crew made them less than appealing to captains. Mowat considered *Albany* seaworthy, although in poor condition.

Henry Mowat would command HMS *Albany* for the next six years. His ship was a 230-ton sloop of war. It was ninety-one feet long with a twenty-six-foot beam and was armed with sixteen cannons. At the time of the Penobscot

HMS *Albany* was ninety-one feet long and was built in New York. It is thought that *Albany* was converted to a warship from the American sloop *Howe. Courtesy of John Flint.*

Expedition in 1779, *Albany* carried a crew of 125 men, although at the time of its fatal accident in 1782, the ship's crew was fewer than sixty men.

For the next four years, the now-infamous captain prowled the New England coast in his refitted sloop of war, preying on American merchant shipping. After the British evacuation from Boston, he took prizes and protected the sea lanes between New York and Halifax. Captain Flint wrote, "Most of the time *Albany* guarded Canadian waters from rebel fishermen, an assignment he found demeaning for one of his seniority and talents."

Although Mowat was described as haughty and having an explosive temper, he was respected by his peers as a good officer. Admiral Shuldham, who replaced Admiral Graves, referred to Mowat as "the most useful person in America under naval authority." A London newspaper hailed his patrol as "the most successful of the fall [1777] season." While on patrol, Mowat had twice confronted John Paul Jones. On the second occasion, he drove the legendary American captain into Boston Harbor after putting his ship *Alfred* out of action.

Life on HMS *Albany*, as on all ships in the Royal Navy, was brutal and hard. On board a small sloop of war patrolling the Maine coast, it was doubly so. The quarters were cramped, with more than one hundred officers and men crowded into dank and dark spaces between the decks.

The Maine winters were especially difficult, with northeast gales, blizzards and the pressure of constant patrolling. The coast was uncharted except for sketches that Mowat had personally made on his many cruises since 1754. It was therefore not unusual for *Albany* to run on unmarked rocks. Mowat would then be forced to seek a sheltered cove, haul his sloop out and have the ship's carpenter make the necessary repairs.

Summers were more bearable. Provisions could be purchased from sympathetic Loyalist farmers, and fresh water was available from the many streams along the coast, as well as wood for the galley range. Hatch covers could be removed, allowing air and sunlight to penetrate below decks. Even Maine tides were helpful. Mowat would run *Albany* ashore at high tide, and when the tide dropped, the crew was put to work scraping away the barnacles and grass fouling the hull. Crew problems were rare since there were few places to run and hide along the lonely, rocky coast.

The Penobscot Expedition

A year into the Revolution, the Royal Navy was dominating the Atlantic seaboard. Over time, however, bad weather and battles with the French navy withered away what one naval historian has called "a vast armada, one of the largest fleet of warships ever seen in North American waters." By 1779, not a single town in New England was in British hands.

The situation was particularly serious at the New York and Halifax dockyards, the only towns where British ships could be refitted. At Halifax, Nova Scotia, *Albany*'s homeport, things were so bad that the effectiveness of the North American Squadron was threatened. Supplies for repair were running low, especially timbers for masts, bowsprits and planking.

Under these deteriorating circumstances, Henry Mowat received orders in 1779 for his first major command since the burning of Falmouth in 1775. He was given a three-ship flotilla with orders to transport elements of two Highland regiments from Halifax to Penobscot Bay. There, he and British general Francis McLean were ordered to build a fort overlooking the entrance to the Penobscot River at present-day Castine. The purpose of the fort would be to secure vital naval stores and timber for the shipyards in New York and Halifax.

A British presence would thus be reestablished that would provide a haven for Loyalists in the region. The fort would also serve as a base for protecting Canadian commerce and fishing from American privateers. The orders pleased General McLean, who wrote, "He would derive much assistance from Mowat's abilities and knowledge of that coast."

Mowat arrived in Halifax on schedule to convoy the expedition. In June 1779, a fleet of three warships and four armed transports, carrying 650 Scots soldiers, set sail from Halifax, with Henry Mowat in command in his flagship *Albany*.

Led by General McLean, the soldiers disembarked on June 17, 1779, and took control of what at that point was a mere hamlet surrounded by several sawmills. A site for a fort was staked out on a commanding rise two hundred feet above sea level, and work was begun. The proposed fort would be named Fort George in honor of King George III.

Professor Stone pointed out that an added advantage was that most of the officers and men were Scots, who were well known for their engineering skills. Located above the village, Fort George was sited so that its guns had an open field of fire in any direction. In the words of George Washington, Fort George became "the most regularly constructed and best finished of any fortress in North America."

Building Fort George turned out to be a race against time. When word of the British occupation of the Pentagoet (Castine) Peninsula reached the Massachusetts Board of War, it realized the strategic importance of the move and ordered that an expeditionary force be dispatched immediately to dislodge the invaders. (Remember, the Province of Maine was part of Massachusetts until 1820.) The British occupation of the peninsula was too important to go uncontested since the area also provided supplies, including valuable sources of timber for the American war effort.

Historians consider the Penobscot Expedition that followed one of the worst naval operations in American history. From the start, the mission was plagued with problems. Dudley Saltonstall, a cranky commodore from Connecticut, was put in command of a fleet of eighteen warships and twenty-four transports. General Solomon Lovell was in charge of one thousand poorly trained and ill-equipped militiamen and four hundred marines. A familiar name, Paul Revere was given command of the artillery. In its anxiety, the Massachusetts War Board gave Saltonstall and Lovell a mere week to get organized. On July 25, the largest amphibious expedition of the American Revolution arrived off Castine.

Meanwhile, British soldiers and American Loyalists living on the Pentagoet Peninsula, also known by its Indian name of Bagaduce, were feverishly clearing the land and constructing a quadrangular fortress made mostly of earth and sod. The earthworks acted as a cushion. In a short siege, they actually made Fort George less vulnerable because cannonballs fired from ships would simply sink into the soil and not send splinters from wood and stone flying in every direction.

Captain Mowat's knowledge of upper Penobscot Bay was proving to be invaluable. Indeed, his reputation had preceded him since it soon was evident that Commodore Saltonstall was intimidated by the very mention of his name. Even though the advancing American fleet mounted 344 guns on eighteen warships and outgunned the British, Saltonstall delayed an attack for several days. As a result, the British were able to continue work on Fort George.

Mowat was later to write, "These three or four days of embarrassment on the part of the rebels gave our troops time to do something more to the fort, to carry up the most necessary stores, and to mount several more guns." During these early days of the siege Mowat "seconded" (sent ashore) sailors under his command to work on the construction of the fort and artillery battery on the peninsula, with one of the batteries being manned by gun crews from his sloops.

To defend the peninsula, Mowat came up with a clever tactic. He strung, or "sprung" (the nautical term), his three sloops bow to stern across the entrance to Castine's harbor. This would force American ships attacking the town to face a concentrated broadside. Mowat next unloaded the guns on

The British fleet seen advancing on Castine. Americans ships are fleeing in the background. *Courtesy of National Maritime Museum, Greenwich, England.*

the off side of his ships and sent them ashore, providing another battery for the defense of the peninsula.

As the combined land-sea American operation was about to be launched, a British relief fleet under Commodore George Collier was spotted heading up Penobscot Bay toward the besieged fort. Collier's flagship, the sixty-four-gun *Raisonable*, was clearly superior to any of the American warships. Although the Americans had more warships and more guns, they quickly realized that they were no match for the better-trained British crews.

The battle was over before it had begun. After exchanging a few rounds with the British, the American warships turned tail and fled up the Penobscot River, followed by twenty-four ungainly transports crammed with troops. The next day, the river was filled with scuttled ships, and the banks were littered with the remains of vessels that had been run ashore and burned.

It took one month for the bedraggled American militiamen to make their way back through the wilderness to Massachusetts. After he returned from the ordeal, American General Lovell was heard to say, "Why couldn't we have fought the way the British did?"

Professor Stone described Henry Mowat as a "heroic figure" in the whole affair. As commander of the three sloops led by HMS *Albany*, he held off an attack on the fort until the British fleet showed up, thus providing a crucial delaying action.

British General McLean provided us with a different view. In his report to the Admiralty, he never mentioned the actions of the three sloops of war during the siege and omitted the names of their captains, most significantly Mowat's. Nor did Commodore Collier's dispatches to London make any mention of the service of Mowat's little fleet. In short, Mowat's superiors agreed with an American historian's version of the affair that "Mowat's contribution to the British victory at Penobscot was negligible." It would appear that Mowat's noncompliance of his orders at Falmouth back in 1775 had not been forgotten by the British high command.

Albany's Final Years

In October 1780, colonists on Islesboro were astonished to see a small boat approaching HMS *Albany*, bearing a flag of truce. On board was a determined young science professor named Fortescue Vernon from Harvard College. The previous summer, Fortescue's mentor, Reverend Professor Williams, realized that an eclipse of the sun would occur in October and would be visible along the eastern coast of Maine, which was then part of Massachusetts. War or no war, the Harvard scientists were determined not to miss it.

Reverend Professor Williams sent Fortescue Vernon and six students to record the event. They arrived at Camden in mid-October carrying a letter from Reverend Williams stating that "their business was solely to promote the interest of Science." Peleg Wadsworth, the American commander, gave them permission to proceed into Penobscot Bay under a flag of truce. *Albany*'s captain, Henry Mowat, was apparently "friendly and courteous," although the Scottish commander, Colonel Campbell, was less welcoming: "Com up ye Bay immediately, anchor ye vessel in Williams Cove...Have no communication with ye inhabitants and depart on ye 28th day of ye month."

A thick Maine fog blanketed the coast for the next week, but on the morning of October 27, the weather cleared, and a perfect day dawned for the viewing. Apparently, the eclipse was "a wondrous experience" for the scientists, who wrote down detailed observations before departing the next day.

In this image from 1980, Harvard astronomy professors Barbara Hughes (second from right) and Gordon Schiff (third from right) are shown displaying the eighteenth-century instruments that were used to measure an eclipse of the sun on Islesboro in 1780. *Courtesy of Islesboro Historical Society.*

HMS *Albany* was wrecked in a winter storm in Penobscot Bay in 1782. *Courtesy of John Flint.*

After serving for twenty-seven years along the North Atlantic coast, Henry Mowat was finally permitted to return to England. Sitting in his chilly London flat, the disaffected officer wrote a twenty-nine-page letter of grievance to the king outlining his frustrations at not receiving faster promotions. Mowat stated that "his feelings as a man, his spirit and honor as an officer and his duty to the service were injured and degraded... Circumstances compel me to consider resignation from the service."

But Mowat did not resign. When he returned to the North American Station, the frustrated officer (he had finally been promoted to captain) was given command of a captured French merchant ship, the twenty-eight-gun *La Sophie*. Years later, Mowat was on patrol off the coast of Virginia when he suffered a fatal stroke on board his current ship *Defiance* in 1798. The sixty-three-year-old sailor was buried at St. John's Cemetery, Hampton, Virginia, where his tombstone can be seen today.

Although he never married, Henry Mowat's will records that he left his estate to a son, William Mowat, and daughter, Mary Ann Mowat. It is thought both were the result of an affair he had with an American woman, although there is no record of who she was.

Mowat was no longer in command of HMS *Albany* in 1782 when it was declared "unfit for further military service," and it was relegated to patrol duty. The frail vessel was caught in a nasty winter storm on December 28, 1782, and ran on one of the Northern Triangle ledges with such force that it was quickly apparent that there was no way of getting it off. Most of the crew managed to get into the ship's two boats, a cutter and a pinnace. The men in the pinnace reached nearby Ash Point, south of Owls Head. There they chartered a boat owned by a man named Captain Haskell that returned to *Albany* and transported the remainder of the crew to Castine.

The cutter got lost in the "vapors" and finally ended up at Markey's Beach on Matinicus Island. By that time, three men had succumbed to the cold. Even today, old-timers still call it "Dead Man's Beach." The survivors were carried ashore, defrosted and treated kindly by island inhabitants.

While treating a young British sailor, one of the local women known as Aunt Susan noticed tears in his eyes. When she questioned him, he admitted that he had been a member of the *Albany* raiding party that had landed on Matinicus a few months previously and killed her cow for food. Even British sailors could show remorse.

In a bit of irony, Cyrus Eaton wrote in his *History of Thomaston* about a local boy, Joshua Thorndike, who had enlisted shortly after the Battle of Bunker Hill. Thorndike had served aboard a privateer from Falmouth that was captured by HMS *Albany*. He was subsequently kept aboard as a prisoner for nine months.

When he heard about the wreck, the delighted Thorndike and two friends sailed out to the scene and proceeded to salvage as much of value as they could before "the detested craft" went to pieces. The cannons, however, fell through the bottom of the boat and remained in the water for the next two hundred years.

Captain John Flint added a final ironic note. In August 1993, he met the diver who had located the cannons, cannonballs and other items from HMS *Albany* amid the rocks of the Northern Triangles. The diver's name was Saltonstall, who was a direct descendant of Dudley Saltonstall, the American commander of the ill-fated Penobscot Expedition.

CAPTAIN MORRIS' MISTAKE: THE FATEFUL CRUISE OF USS *ADAMS*

On the western end of Isle au Haut in Penobscot Bay, there is a place known locally as "Captain Morris' Mistake." During the War of 1812, following an escape from two British frigates, the twenty-eight-gun American corvette *Adams*, commanded by Charles Morris, ran on a ledge in the fog. Although many in the ship's crew were ill with scurvy, the healthy men saved the ship by removing its guns. The now lightened *Adams* was pulled off and retreated up the Penobscot River.

An Intrepid Young Naval Officer

Charles Morris is one of the lesser-known but daring young naval officers to emerge from the War of 1812. Morris entered the United States Navy in 1799 as an acting midshipman and advanced rapidly through the ranks. He became a lieutenant at twenty-three and was appointed a captain at twenty-eight. During the First Barbary War (1801–5), Morris served under the irascible Commodore Edward Preble, from whom he learned how important it was to obey orders "to preserve a favorable opinion," as he wrote in his *Autobiography*.

Morris's initial moment of glory came in 1804 when he was selected to participate in a daring raid to destroy USS *Philadelphia*, which had

Charles Morris was a bold
United States naval officer who
fought in the War of 1812.
Courtesy of Harold van Doren.

grounded in Tripoli Harbor and had been captured by the forces of Pasha
Yusuf Karamanli. The expedition was led by Stephen Decatur, who sailed
a captured enemy ketch into Tripoli Harbor and set fire to *Philadelphia*
before the enemy was able to react. Morris led the boarding party to
destroy the stricken ship. In his *Autobiography*, Morris proudly reported,
"The success of this enterprise added much to the reputation of the Navy
both at home and abroad."

In January 1812, shortly before war between the United States and
Great Britain, Morris met Napoleon while in France. His description of the
Emperor is worth noting:

> *The object of interest was Napoleon himself, but it is difficult to describe
> his appearance and the expression of his countenance. In height, he was
> about five feet, eight inches.* [He was actually five feet, two inches.]
> *He had already exchanged the slight and slender figure of the conqueror of
> Italy for a fullness, which verged closely upon corpulence. His movements
> were slow, but easy and dignified.*

When the War of 1812 broke out in June of that year, Morris was first lieutenant of USS *Constitution*. The next month, *Constitution* was becalmed off the New Jersey shore when a British squadron of five warships spotted it and immediately gave chase. Captain Isaac Hull followed a suggestion made by Morris, which was to put the ship's boats over the side and, by a technique called warping or kedging*, pull the ship out of range. Slowly, *Constitution* pulled away, although the British ships soon adopted the same technique. After fifty-seven exhausting hours, the British finally abandoned the chase, whereby *Constitution* was able to escape, having lightened itself by pumping 2,300 gallons of drinking water overboard.

The next month, *Constitution* engaged the British frigate *Guerriere* in single-ship combat that turned out to be a one-sided contest. Within thirty minutes, *Guerriere* was reduced to what George Daughan in *1812: The Navy's War* called "a floating log, whereas *Constitution* was practically unscathed." Charles Morris, however, was not unscathed. Although badly wounded, he remained on deck in the thick of the fight. In his report to navy secretary Paul Hamilton, Captain Hull credited Morris as being a key to the victory.

Morris was put ashore in Boston to recover from his wounds, while *Constitution* sailed off into naval history, defeating one British ship after another. During the course of the battle with *Guerriere*, British cannonballs appeared to bounce off *Constitution*'s oak hull, giving rise to the venerable ship's nickname, "Old Ironsides."

Kedging is to move, or warp, a vessel forward by means of a line attached to an anchor that is dropped from a small boat.

The Captain of USS *Adams*

Morris was rewarded for his bravery during the battle with *Guerriere* with promotion to the rank of captain by Secretary of the Navy Hamilton. He candidly wrote in his *Autobiography*:

> This unexpected advancement over a whole grade, which had only the precedent of Decatur, was considered by some beyond my merits; by still more, as an injudicious departure from the usual routine; and by all those over whom I had been advanced, as fully justifying all their exertions to prevents its confirmation by the Senate. It was quite as unexpected by me as by anyone, and I should have felt well satisfied if promoted to master-commander [the next level of command].

Although he was well liked, some of Morris's fellow officers had protested to Secretary Hamilton for his seemingly impulsive promotion of the young lieutenant. George Daughan called it "an unnecessary blow to the morale of the entire officer corps and one more example of Hamilton's ineptness." Hamilton would resign by the end of the year.

Morris was given command of USS *Adams* in May 1813, a small frigate that he soon found unstable and a poor sailing craft. The ship was built in Brooklyn, New York, in 1798 and was apparently the first warship built by the newly formed United States Navy. According to one report, half its hull had been subcontracted to a builder who scrimped on materials. The result was that *Adams* ended up shorter on one side than the other, which meant it sailed better on one tack than the other.

Morris protested that *Adams* "was insufficient for sea service," to which a survey by a board of naval officers agreed. The conversion to a twenty-eight-gun corvette (a sloop of war), however, took several months, and it was not until 1814 that *Adams* was able to put to sea. Then there was the problem of the British blockade. Morris wrote that "the enemy were constantly in force near the outlet of the bay [Chesapeake] and there was no chance for our getting past them undiscovered."

In the middle of January 1814, Morris finally had a chance to run his new command past the British blockade. At the entrance to the bay, he wrote that "we struck ground two or three times but then suddenly she was free." Two enemy ships spotted *Adams*, but moving at twelve and a half knots, the corvette quickly raced past them. Its new captain was thoroughly pleased: "When daylight broke upon us, neither enemy nor land was in sight."

Morris sailed *Adams* across the Atlantic to the Canaries and the Cape Verde Islands in search of prizes. En route, they captured three small brigs, two of which they destroyed. "On our return passage," Morris wrote, "we had just taken possession of a ship from India with a cargo of rice when we were discovered by two ships of war guarding a convoy of twenty-five ships. We were compelled to recall our men, relinquish the ship and attend to our own safety."

On May 1, 1814, Morris recorded, "We arrived at the mouth of the Savannah River nearly destitute of provisions and water." Unfortunately, the depth was too shallow for his ship to proceed the fifteen miles upriver to Savannah to resupply. He was able to load a few provisions from nearby American ships at the river's mouth before a British frigate spotted him. Morris again used the warping/kedging technique to get his ship out of the Savannah River and begin the next leg of his cruise.

Still on the prowl for prizes, Morris headed for Ireland, where, he despaired, "We saw not a single vessel." On the return voyage, *Adams* had just destroyed two brigs when it was spotted by the thirty-six-gun British frigate *Tigris*, which immediately gave chase. During the pursuit, Morris ordered that several cannons and two anchors be thrown overboard to lighten the ship. "The next day a good breeze soon enabled us to leave our pursuer, the ship making thirty-one miles in three hours."

Passing Newfoundland, Morris encountered two more British frigates that immediately sped after him. One soon gave up the chase. Morris later wrote, "The other, however, continued for forty hours during time which we ran four hundred miles of latitude, without perceptibly increasing the distance between the ships." *Adams* finally escaped during the second night by changing course several times, "by which we lost sight of her."

By mid-August 1814, the cruise of USS *Adams* had lasted for seven months. Provisions were desperately low, and cases of scurvy were breaking out among the crew, as well as a number of enemy prisoners on board. Morris would later recall, "Our expectations had been greatly disappointed, for we had anticipated active and successful employment so near the coasts and harbors of the enemy; and now we were about to return without either profit or fame which afforded us little satisfaction."

Captain Morris was now faced with a choice. He could remain at sea and continue to look for more prizes, or he could head for the safe port of Portsmouth, New Hampshire, attend to the sick on board (there were now fifty-eight cases of scurvy) and re-provision his ship. To do this, however, he risked an encounter with enemy shipping. An even greater problem was a lack of charts for the Maine coast. Clayton Gross, in *Island Chronicles: Deer Isle & Stonington*, reminded that "[l]ighthouses did not appear in Penobscot Bay until 1820–1840." After weighing the risks, Morris decided to head for Portsmouth.

The Final Days of USS *Adams*

Deer Isle historian Clayton Gross described what happened next. "While bowling along at ten knots off the back side of Isle au Haut, the *Adams* ran hard aground on a rock." Foggy weather had prevented an accurate observation of *Adam's* position for several days. Soundings, however, seemed to confirm that they were about sixty miles from Cape Ann, which was actually well to the south. Fearing an encounter with blockading British

Cliffs on the Western Ear of Isle au Haut. USS *Adams* ran on Flat Ledge one hundred yards offshore from these bluffs. *Author's collection.*

ships, prisoners had been placed in the hold. Suddenly, the forward lookout yelled, "Breakers," and the ship struck.

It was 4:00 a.m. on the morning of August 17 when Captain Morris rushed on deck to survey the damage. USS *Adams* had run up on a rock, which had lifted its bow about six feet out of the water. Boats were immediately hoisted out, since Morris was under the false impression that they had hit the dangerous shoals of Cashe's Ledge, eighty miles east of Cape Ann. When dawn broke, everyone was relieved to see a landing place below a high cliff, although their exact location on the coast was still unclear.

The sick were landed on a nearby rocky beach along with a medical officer, and a tent of sails was erected. The question of prisoners remained a problem. This was resolved when Captain Morris found Richard Knowlton, a local fisherman, to take them to Thomaston. En route, apparently, there was an attempt to escape. George Hosmer in a *Historical Sketch of Deer Isle* described what happened next: "Mr. Knowlton and his brother Robert were very resolute and gave them to understand that it

The rocky beach where the wounded from USS *Adams* were taken before being transported to Thomaston. *Author's collection.*

would not be safe for them to undertake it. They then became quiet and were carried to their place of destination."

Efforts were made to lighten the stricken *Adams* by removing the guns, while at the same time working the pumps vigorously, since water was rising in the hull. After several hours, the ship was finally refloated on an incoming tide, although it was clear that repairs were needed before *Adams* was serviceable. Morris wrote, "We were now once more safe from the dangers of the shore, but ignorant of our position and we were liable to meet with enemies who we supposed to be cruising in our vicinity."

Once off the rock, today known as Flat Ledge, Morris spent the next day sailing his ship through the fog around what he would eventually realize was Penobscot Bay. Clayton Gross told us that the sixteen-gun British sloop HMS *Rifleman* was sighted southwest of Saddleback Ledge, but *Adams* was able to slip away. The next morning, the fog finally lifted, and the weather was bright and sunny. "Land was in sight," Morris observed, "but, to our surprise, it showed we were nearer Mount Desert, instead of in the neighborhood of Portsmouth."

During the course of running from *Rifleman*, the leak in *Adams*'s hull worsened, and Morris realized that he needed to find a secure port for repairs. Under normal circumstances, the twenty-eight-gun *Adams* was more than a match for the little sloop, but Morris feared that cannon fire would worsen the leaks in his ship's hull.

On the evening of August 19, *Adams* entered the Penobscot River and proceeded twenty miles upstream to the village of Hampden, just south of Bangor. At the same time, Morris "was gratified by the information that our sick had been safely conveyed to Camden" and that the prisoners were secure in Thomaston.

Adams's days were numbered, however. The sloop HMS *Rifleman* had notified the British blockading squadron that an American ship was in the area, and an advance up the Penobscot River was organized. Hearing of this, as Morris wrote in his *Autobiography*,

> [t]*he ship was dismantled, her armament and stores landed, and the preparations were in progress for heaving the ship out to ascertain and, if possible, repair her injuries, when intelligence was received by express that sixteen of the enemy's vessels had entered the bay. They had captured Castine, thirty miles below us, and their immediate advance up the river was contemplated.*

The Battle of Hampden

Morris requested assistance, and to his delight, nearly four hundred militia from nearby Brewer, along with thirty regular troops, appeared. Using the guns from his ship, Morris's men "by great exertions placed nine of our guns in two batteries upon an adjoining hill, but without much protection." At the same time, he made plans to destroy his ship if it became necessary. Meanwhile, a large British force, in ten transports, accompanied by two sloops, sailed upriver to Winterport, where they disembarked and marched to Hampden.

The so-called Battle of Hampden was fought at dawn on the morning of September 2, 1814, and was over in one hour. At the sound of enemy bugles, a force of British regulars advanced on the local militia supported by thirty marines. After a few exchanges of gunfire, the American ranks broke and fled in disorder.

Realizing that they were about to be outflanked and that the American cause was hopeless, Morris reluctantly gave the order to spike the cannons to prevent them from falling into enemy hands. In his *Autobiography*, he bemoaned "the absence of preparations before the enemy appeared, and the failure of the militia to make any resistance." Finally, Morris ordered USS *Adams* to be destroyed to keep it from being captured by the British.

George Wasson, in *Sailing Days on the Penobscot*, described the British response:

> *Angered by this and by the show of resistance offered by the militia at Hampden, the English sacked the village and continued to Bangor. Here, eight vessels on the stocks were at once burned and six more were loaded with provisions for the garrison at Castine. Bangor was itself only spared on the most humiliating terms of ransom.*

The British then withdrew to Castine, where they remained until war ended in the spring of 1815. Morris and his men marched on a newly made road (more likely a trail) through the wilderness from Bangor to Canaan, on the Kennebec River. At Canaan, Morris borrowed funds from the Bank of Waterville to feed his crew. The entire company then proceeded to the naval base at Portsmouth, New Hampshire, where they reported to the commanding officer, Commodore Isaac Hull. During the entire trek of two hundred miles, Morris proudly reported not one man deserted and none died.

A Court of Inquiry was ordered that fully exonerated the officers and crew for the loss of USS *Adams*, along with some compliments on their general good conduct. "Thus terminated my first command," Morris wrote candidly in his *Autobiography*. "Not only had all our expectations of gaining reputation by an important success been disappointed, but our ship had been lost and a formal inquiry held to ascertain if punishment was deserved."

George Daughan offered a critical view: "In spite of all his efforts, Morris' cruise had been an abysmal failure. He did capture ten vessels, but they were of no importance. Of far greater consequence was the loss of one of the country's few warships and an inordinate number of men as a result of scurvy."

Isle au Haut writer Harold van Doren added some final thoughts regarding the corvette USS *Adams*:

> *The hull of the Adams lay in the Hampden mud for fifty-six years, pretty much ignored except for wreckers who peeled copper off her bottom when it was exposed by the tides. But in 1870 she was raised.*

Years later, USS *Adams* was rebuilt using the original hull. It is seen here as a steam sloop in the 1870s. *Courtesy of Harold Van Doren.*

Her hull of solid oak was relatively undamaged, even after being blown up, and she was taken to Boston and rebuilt. She then served as a U.S. Navy training ship, the last sailing vessel to be used for that purpose. She made voyages all over the world including Alaska and Hawaii. About 1920 she was reportedly broken up at the advanced age of a hundred and twenty-four years.

There are several similarities between the destruction of USS *Adams* and the ill-fated Penobscot Expedition in 1779. Both involved the flight of American warships up the Penobscot River in the face of an overwhelming British force and the retreat by hundreds of men through a wilderness to the Kennebec River. Of course, the Penobscot Expedition was a disaster of the first magnitude for the United States Navy, whereas USS *Adams* was only a single ship commanded by a brave, if unlucky, captain.

Postwar Morris

Shortly before the War of 1812 ended, Charles Morris was given command of the frigate USS *Congress*, which was "gratifying to my feelings" and proof that the navy still believed in him. Morris spent twenty-one of his fifty-seven-year naval career serving on American warships around the world. He was appointed to the Board of Naval Commissioners in 1820, which had been established to aid the secretary of the navy with his responsibilities. As such, Morris had a voice in important questions of naval administration for the next twelve years.

Captain Morris was selected in 1825 by President John Quincy Adams to command the frigate USS *Brandywine* to return the Marquis de Lafayette to France after his triumphant tour celebrating the fiftieth anniversary of the founding of the United States.

Charles Morris suffered from ill health throughout his life, although he lived to the age of seventy-one. When he died in 1856, the son of the great Civil War Admiral David Farragut, Loyall Farragut, was quoted as saying, "My father was a great admirer of Commodore Morris, and has alluded to him in his journal as 'the ablest sea officer of his day.'"

THE CONFEDERATE RAIDER: CSS *GEORGIA*

CSS *Georgia* was one of the lesser-known members of the diminutive Confederate navy. The iron-framed ship was built in 1862 in Dumbarton, Scotland, and was designed as a merchant vessel before it was refitted as one of twelve Confederate commerce raiders. Originally named *Japan*, *Georgia* was secretly purchased by the Confederacy in March 1863, even though there were doubts as to whether iron-bottomed ships were suited for long cruises in the days before antifouling paint.

Following the Civil War, *Georgia* was reconfigured for freight and passenger service and spent ten years sailing the East Coast of the United States and the Maritime Provinces. After a disaster in the St. Lawrence River in 1874, it was put on the Halifax-Portland run. The former raider met its end in a winter storm in 1875 when it ran on the ledges of the Northern Triangles in Penobscot Bay near Tenants Harbor.

Getting Started

By the middle of the Civil War, the supposedly neutral British government had become extremely sensitive about selling ships to the Confederacy. When *Japan* set sail in April 1863, it was reputedly on a voyage to Singapore. Off the coast of France, however, the ship rendezvoused with the small steamer *Alar*, where it took on guns, ordnance and other stores. The Confederate flag was raised, and *Japan* was recommissioned as CSS *Georgia*. Lieutenant William Lewis Maury, who had gone along as a member of the fifty-man crew, was placed in command with orders to prey on United States merchant ships wherever they could be found.

When the Civil War broke out, 247 officers in the United States Navy resigned their commissions and joined the Southern cause. The result was that the Confederate navy was put together in a remarkably short period of time. Two months before war began, the Confederate Congress created a Navy Department. As I wrote in my book *Mainers in the Civil War*:

> *It should be noted, however, that the Confederate Navy operated at a huge disadvantage throughout the war. In April 1861, the North had forty-two commissioned warships; the Confederacy had none. With few exceptions, the South was therefore forced to wage a defensive war. Southern privateers were called commerce raiders and their objective was to disrupt the North's merchant fleet as much as possible.*

Much of what we know about CSS *Georgia* as a commerce raider is from a book by James Morris Morgan, *Recollections of a Rebel Reefer*, published when he was seventy-two in 1917. *Georgia* was not a large warship. It was a bit over two hundred feet long and weighed six hundred tons. The ship was described by Morgan as a "poor, miserable little tin kettle of a craft," but, he added, "I loved her."

The "miserable little tin kettle" was armed with two one-hundred-pound cannons, two twenty-four-pound cannons and a single thirty-two-pound rifled Whitworth gun. With a top speed of thirteen knots, the coal-burning *Georgia* was essentially a steamship with auxiliary sails.

Because of the war, the ship's captain, William Maury, was restricted to coaling at neutral ports. As a result, *Georgia* spent a good deal of time under sail with its boilers banked. At the same time, Maury was constantly on the lookout for unsuspecting Northern ships carrying loads of coal.

Left: Lieutenant William Lewis Maury was commander of the Confederate raider CSS *Georgia*. His orders were to attack Union merchant ships around the world. *From the collections of James Morris Morgan.*

Below: CSS *Georgia* was built in England as a steamship with axillary sails. It was slightly over two hundred feet long and weighed six hundred tons. *Courtesy of Library of Congress, Prints and Photographs Division.*

George Trenholm was a wealthy South Carolina businessman whose firm became the Confederate government's overseas banker. *From the collections of James Morris Morgan.*

James Morgan grew up in New Orleans, the youngest of nine children. At the age of fifteen, he was admitted to the Naval Academy in 1860. "Youngster you are all right," a gruff senior officer told the nervous boy. Morgan trained on the historic old frigate *Constitution* while suffering through the rigors of a northern winter. As the nation drifted toward war, the young southerner recorded, "By the end of 1860 a dark cloud had settled over our spirits and we spent our leisure moments discussing the burning question of secession."

With the firing on Fort Sumter, Midshipman Morgan resigned from the navy "with a lump in my throat" and headed home, where he was "most heartily welcomed." He met Thomas Huger, captain of a Confederate sloop of war, who accepted him as a member of the crew when he learned that Morgan had studied at Annapolis. Morgan spent the next two years serving on various Southern warships on the East Coast and in the Gulf of Mexico.

One evening in October 1862, Morgan was at a party with a group of friends in Charleston, South Carolina, when a wealthy businessman, George Trenholm, asked him "if he would like to go abroad and join a cruiser. I told him nothing would delight me more." The next day, he was handed a telegram. "Report to Commodore Matthew F. Maury for duty abroad, Mr. Trenholm will arrange for your passage." The telegram was signed by Secretary of the Navy Stephen R. Mallory. "It fairly took my breath away," wrote young Morgan.

There were actually two Maurys connected with USS *Georgia*. Commodore Matthew F. Maury was a distinguished United States naval officer, and the aforementioned Lieutenant William Maury was his nephew. Previously,

Midshipman James Morris Morgan's autobiography, *Recollections of a Rebel Reefer*, provides us with much of what we know about the cruise of CSS *Georgia*. From the collections of James Morris Morgan.

William Maury had achieved prominence as a naval officer as commander of USS *Saratoga* during Commodore Perry's expedition to Japan in 1854.

At the start of the war, both men resigned their commissions in the United States Navy and joined the Confederate navy. The senior Maury soon became a critic of Secretary of the Navy Stephen Mallory. To keep him occupied, the harassed secretary sent the contentious commodore to England, where he was ordered to procure ships and supplies for the Southern cause.

Meanwhile, the younger Maury was stationed in Charleston, where he was in charge of mining the harbor to keep out Union warships. In December 1862, William was sent "on vacation" to Scotland. In reality, he was carrying negotiable securities for his uncle that would enable him to purchase ships. The expectation was that his nephew would be given command of one of the ships.

Midshipman James Morris was involved with both Maurys. He sailed to England as an aide to Commodore Matthew Maury in the fall of 1862. They stopped first in Bermuda, where they were forced to wait until a British sloop of war arrived to escort them past two lurking Northern warships. Morgan's impressions of Maury are worth noting:

> *Commodore Maury was a deeply religious man. He had been lame for many years but no one ever heard him complain. He was also the only man I ever saw who could be seasick and amiable at the same time; while*

suffering from nausea he could actually joke! Not knowing of his worldwide celebrity I was surprise to see the deference paid to him by foreigners.

Morgan described his life in England during the winter of 1862–63 as "a lonely one" while he waited for his future ship to be readied. Under the name *Japan*, the future Confederate raider finally cleared customs on April 1, 1863, and slipped down the Firth of Clyde. Three days later, it met the tug *Alar*; as Morgan wrote, "we worked like beavers" to transfer the guns and other ordinance in what he describes as a heavy sea.

CSS *Georgia* was not an easy ship to sail, according to Morgan:

She lay very low in the water and was very long for her beam. Her sail power was insufficient, and, owing to her length, it was impossible to put her about under canvas. She was slow under either sail or steam, or both together. Such was the little craft in which we got slowly under way, bound we know not where.

The Cruise of CSS *Georgia*

CSS *Georgia* set a course for the South Atlantic. During the course of the next eight months, it would capture and destroy nine Northern vessels with a combined value of more than $4 million. The first prize was *Dictator*, sighted on April 25, 1863, carrying a cargo of coal. Attempts were made to transfer the fuel, but "the rising sea made this impossible; and after coming very near swamping our small boats, we gave it up." Morgan wrote:

Dictator's crew was taken prisoner and the coal ship was burned. Midshipman Morgan was unable to get the fire started until a superior officer "showed him how it was done. By the time we got back to Georgia [Morgan does not include "CSS" when referring to Georgia], the prize was a seething mass of flames." Dictator, exclusive of her cargo, was worth $86,000 in prize money. The Confederate government had announced that the crew would receive half the value of every ship destroyed.

CSS *Georgia* reached the Brazilian port of Bahia in early May and dropped anchor next to the famed Confederate raider *Alabama*, fresh off a victory over USS *Hatteras*. Maury's crew was given a firsthand account of the battle, and prisoners from *Dictator* were put ashore. Because he was fluent

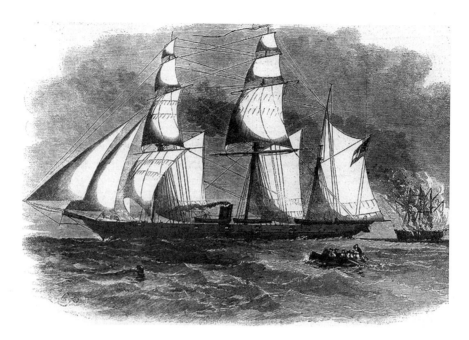

The famed Confederate raider *Alabama* is seen having set fire to a Union merchant ship. Morgan met *Alabama*'s Captain Raphael Semmes in the Brazilian port of Bahia. *Courtesy of Library of Congress, Prints and Photographs Division.*

in French, Morgan related that he was used as a translator by *Alabama*'s Captain Semmes to communicate with the governor of Bahia, "who like most educated South Americans, spoke French perfectly."

"Chasing ships without making any captures was getting to be a little monotonous," Morgan wrote. After two months of futile pursuits, CSS *Georgia* finally captured the merchant ship *Constitution* off the coast of Trinidad. The vessel was from Philadelphia, bound for Shanghai with a cargo of coal and missionaries. Bringing the missionaries on board was easy, but it took several days to transfer the coal, "which was a weary job as our boats were small." Shortly after this, Morgan related, the crew heard the sad news of the death of "Stonewall" Jackson from a passing neutral ship.

CSS *Georgia* then crossed the Atlantic and arrived at Cape Town in mid-August. The now eighteen-year-old Morgan reported:

> *I lived a simple life owing to the fact that we had not entered a port where anything could be bought for so long a time. I had only my ship's ration of*

salt horse and hard tack to eat, but it must have been a healthful regimen as I had grown wonderfully in height and strength. My sobriquet of "Little Morgan" had become a misnomer.

At Cape Town, the raider was laid up for repairs, and several members of the crew asked to leave the ship. Probably the greatest losses were the engineer and the first officer. Morgan especially regretted the departure of First Lieutenant Chapman. "He was a man of iron nerve, a strict disciplinarian with a kind heart, and absolutely just. It was a bad day for our ship when he left."

Having been cooped up for weeks, Morgan was able to obtain leave and went off to Cape Town to do a bit of sightseeing. Some Union officers, whose ships had been destroyed by the notorious *Alabama*, spotted him in his Confederate uniform. When Morgan entered a hotel dining room later in the day, "they arose en masse, damning pirates in general and myself in particular." Fortunately for Morgan, the hotel's proprietor stepped in and whisked the young Confederate to safety.

Morgan's observations on the treacherous cape weather are also worth mentioning:

One afternoon I asked permission to go ashore and it was granted on my solemn promise that I be back in time to stand watch. I had a most enjoyable time until I had to catch the Georgia's boat when I was disappointed to find that there was no boat for me because it was blowing "great guns." I wanted to keep my promise, but none of the native watermen would take me aboard saying that the sea was too high.

Morgan finally found some Malay fishermen whom he paid an exorbitant sum if they would take him through the heavy surf out to his ship. "Outside the breakers the seas were still higher." Just as they reached the "wallowing and plunging" CSS *Georgia*, the Malay craft sank. Everyone was hoisted safely on board, but Morgan admitted, "The captain gave me a good scolding for what he termed my foolhardiness."

On October 9, after a "lively chase," CSS *Georgia* captured the Northern ship *Bold Hunter*, bound for Calcutta and carrying a full load of coal. Attempts were made to transfer the fuel, but high winds and heavy seas forced them to stop. Reluctantly, Captain Maury gave the order to burn the prize. Morgan described what happened next:

The wind by this time had increased to a gale and the sea was running very high. Like a mad bull the floating inferno bore down on us at full speed rushing through the water as though she was bent on having her revenge. Before we could make sail the burning ship was upon us; we were barely one-sixth her size. The force of the impact pushed us ahead and then we were struck again in the same place.

Despite heroic work by the ship's carpenters, CSS *Georgia* continued to leak badly. The ship limped northward to the Canary Islands, where the latest prisoners were put ashore and emergency repairs were quickly made.

The waters around the Canary Islands were one of the favorite hunting grounds for American whalers, who, in turn, were preyed on by Southern raiders. This caused the area to be frequented by Union warships looking for Southern warships. In fact, a Union vessel had left shortly before their arrival that "would have been the end of *Georgia*'s cruise," Morgan wryly commented.

The raider's eight-month voyage was nearing its end. Captain Maury had been in poor health since they had left Cape Town. (He later described his ailment as "inflammatory rheumatism" in a letter to his wife.) Maury had heard that his wife and children in Richmond had become refugees, and he did not know where they were.

Morgan described Maury as "melancholy." He spent most of the time in his cabin with the ship's doctor, rarely appearing on deck. Morgan also observed that the ship missed the strict discipline of First Lieutenant Chapman. At one point, the crew broke into the liquor stores, causing turmoil that the ship's officers had difficulty in quelling.

With a badly fouled hull, "*Georgia* dragged her heavy crop of grass" up the English Channel to Cherbourg, France, where it was blockaded in by the conqueror of *Alabama*, USS *Kearsarge*. Captain Maury was relieved of his command, and the officers, including Morgan, headed for a well-deserved leave in Paris.

Three months later, in February 1864, with a newly clean bottom, CSS *Georgia* slipped past the blockade and out of Cherbourg. Off Cape Trafalgar, in southern Spain, they ran into a bad storm. According to Morgan, "it was the most terrific in my seafaring experience." The raider then proceeded along the coast of North Africa, where Morgan described an encounter with local Moors that nearly resulted in the loss of the ship.

Late in the spring of 1864, CSS *Georgia* returned to Liverpool, where it was decided that, due to deficiencies in speed and fighting ability, the ship's days as a commerce raider were over. All hands were summoned on deck. After thirty thousand miles of cruising, the Confederate flag was hauled down and the crew paid off.

On June 1, 1864, over the protests of United States Ambassador to Great Britain Charles Francis Adams, *Georgia* was sold to a British merchant. The businessman, whose name was Jones, signed an agreement with Portugal for his new ship to carry the mail between Lisbon and the Cape Verde Islands. When *Georgia* arrived off the Tagus River, however, it was captured by the Northern warship *Niagara* and sent to the United States as a prize. (Mr. Jones was never compensated for the loss of his ship.)

James Morgan provided us with an epitaph for the Confederate commerce raider:

> *The damage done to the North by these little cruisers should not be estimated simply by the number of ships they captured. The Confederate Navy struck the North such a vital blow, by destroying their mercantile marine, that although half a century has elapsed since the scenes I have described took place, the United States has not yet recovered her lucrative carrying trade on the high seas.*

The Wreck of *Georgia*

As a United States ship, *Georgia* was documented as a merchant vessel, and for the next five years, it carried cargo out of New Bedford, Massachusetts. James Morgan remembered seeing the ship in 1866 when he was in Charleston: "I don't believe she had been painted since I left her in Liverpool and she looked like any other dirty old tramp steamer."

Georgia's end was approaching. The ship was reregistered in Canada in 1870 and transported freight and passengers from the Maritime Provinces to Quebec. In the winter of 1874, *Georgia* was trapped in the ice in the St. Lawrence River and sank. It was refloated, repaired and put on the presumably safer run from Halifax to Portland, Maine.

The Northern Triangles are a formidable series of submerged ledges that form the eastern side of Two Bush Channel on the edge of Penobscot Bay. The rocks are barely visible at low tide, and they have claimed more than one unwary vessel, including HMS *Albany*, whose demise was described earlier in this chapter.

The final voyage of *Georgia* began on January 13, 1875, when the ship left Halifax en route to Portland. Under the command of Captain Angrove, the elderly vessel proceeded across the Gulf of Maine carrying twelve passengers. The ship passed north of Matinicus Island in Penobscot Bay, heading for Two Bush Channel. Meanwhile, a heavy snowstorm had developed that forced Captain Angrove to stop the steamer several times to check his position. When *Georgia's* location still was not clear, Angrove stopped again while he and the pilot discussed their options.

Georgia drifted for an hour until, at the pilot's urging, they decided to get underway in the middle of the night instead of waiting for daylight. David Gamage from Jay, Maine, described what happened next:

> *Within ten minutes of getting underway, at about midnight, the iron hull of Georgia slid onto the jagged protruding rocks of the Northern Triangles. The ship came to a stop with half her length aground. With the tide high and beginning to ebb there was no hope of backing off. The seas were running high and with the continual pounding on the ledge the hull soon began to leak profusely and then broke up.*

Captain Angrove launched four lifeboats, and they headed for Tenants Harbor, seven miles away, finally arriving at 7:00 a.m. One of the lifeboats had fouled in the davits, causing six men, including the pilot, to be left on the stricken ship. On the way to Tenants Harbor, one of the lifeboats stopped at the Whitehead Lifesaving Station to inform Keeper Norton of the accident. A surfboat was immediately sent to rescue those left on board.

Heavy seas were running, and the surfboat had to approach the wreck cautiously as it was lodged among the extensive ledges. With each approach, one man was able to drop into the rescue boat until all were saved. An article in the *New York Times* the next day reported, "Six persons left on the steamer were rescued by the life-boat from Whitehead. No lives have been lost, but the steamer *Georgia* is a total loss."

Epilogue

Commodore Matthew Fontaine Maury achieved international acclaim as a naval scholar, teacher and writer before the war. He was nicknamed "Pathfinder of the Seas" and the "Father of Modern Oceanography." Following the war, Maury accepted a teaching position at Virginia Military Institute. He died in 1873 after completing an exhausting lecture tour on international and national weather forecasting.

After the war, James Morgan served as a colonel in the Egyptian army. *From the collections of James Morris Morgan.*

William Lewis Maury, Matthew's nephew, returned to Richmond in 1864. He found his wife and family but had difficulty finding a job after the war. He was finally employed as a customs collector in the Port of New York. He died in Virginia in 1878 at the age of sixty-five.

James Morris Morgan served as a colonel in the Egyptian army after the war and later worked on the construction of the Statue of Liberty. A successful businessman, he was appointed consul general for Australasia (Australia, New Zealand and New Guinea) from 1885 to 1888 by President Grover Cleveland. Morgan was married three times and died in 1928. His delightful autobiography, *Recollections of a Rebel Reefer*, was published in 1917.

THE SINKING OF USS *EAGLE 56*: A COVERUP?

In the final days of World War II, a German submarine crept close to a twenty-five-year-old navy sub chaser a few miles off the coast of Maine. The elderly craft was towing a target buoy for naval aircraft bombing exercises. On April 23, 1945, three miles southeast of Cape Elizabeth, *U-853* fired a torpedo that struck USS *Eagle 56* amidships, breaking it in half and causing an explosion that was heard in Portland nine miles away. Of the sixty-two men on board the old vessel, forty-nine died in the explosion or drowned in the frigid waters of the Gulf of Maine.

As Stephen Puleo related in his powerful and comprehensive book *Due to Enemy Action*, the United States Navy was mortified by an attack that took place so near to the coast and shortly before the anticipated German

Left: John Scagnelli was the engineering officer on USS *Eagle 56*. He had recently supervised the overhauling of the ship's engines in Rockland, Maine. *Courtesy of Stephen Puleo.*

Below: USS *Eagle*'s "Black Gang" (engine room crewmen), seen in Key West the summer before the ship departed for Portland, Maine. *Courtesy of Stephen Puleo.*

surrender; it took fifty-six years for the truth to be revealed. The year after the war ended, a naval board of inquiry announced that the USS *Eagle 56* was sunk due to an explosion of a faulty boiler.

There were thirteen survivors of the disaster, including twenty-five-year-old Lieutenant John Scagnelli, the only officer not killed in the attack. Scagnelli was *Eagle's* engineering officer and had supervised a major overhauling of the ship's boilers and engines while *Eagle 56* was dry-docked in Rockland a short time earlier, thus providing us with a Penobscot Bay connection.

Eagle 56 was the last American warship to be sunk by a U-boat in World War II. The sinking, within sight of the Maine coast, was also the greatest single loss of life to occur in New England waters during World War II. If publicly acknowledged, this would have been a major embarrassment for the navy.

As a result, it is probable that the verdict of a boiler explosion was decided on even before a naval board of inquiry met. Whether it was a deliberate coverup is another matter. Regardless of the navy's motivation behind the decision, to the remaining members of the crew, the finding was nonsense. In fact, some of the survivors claimed to have seen the outline of a submarine as they were leaving their stricken vessel.

The Career of USS *Eagle 56*

History reminds us that German submarine warfare was one of the chief reasons for the United States' entry into World War I. In 1918, the U.S. government contracted with the Ford Motor company to build one hundred Patrol Escort (PE) boats. According to a newspaper article, the designation "Eagle" was used to describe the vessels, "as eagles to scour the seas and pounce on every submarine that dared to leave German shores." The boats were to be two hundred feet long with a thirty-three-foot beam.

Only sixty of the PE boats were ever launched. According to maritime historian Samuel Eliot Morison, they failed as sub chasers and "were almost completely useless." By the outbreak of World War II, only eight of the ships remained in service. *Eagle 56* spent most of the years between the two world wars as a Naval Reserve Training vessel in Baltimore.

During the early years of World War II, *Eagle 56* was used as a training ship at a sonar school in Key West, Florida. Toward the end of the war, it was assigned to the port of Portland, Maine, where its primary function was to tow floating targets for marine bomber pilots. As the war drew to

USS *Eagle 56* was a twenty-five-year-old navy submarine chaser that was sunk off the coast of Maine at the end of World War II. *Courtesy of Stephen Puleo.*

a close, members of *Eagle*'s crew congratulated themselves on having a "cushy job." "What could be safer than Portland Harbor?" a crewmember wrote to his sister.

The seas were moderate at noon on April 23, 1945, when, inexplicably, *Eagle 56* came to a complete stop in the middle of its towing exercises. John Scagnelli was resting in his bunk when he felt the ship halt. Stephen Puleo wrote in his book, "Even with the ship so close to shore, even as war's end approached, this violated naval regulations, and more importantly, rendered the *Eagle* an easy target for any German submarines still in the area."

In fact, United States intelligence records have since revealed that there was a U-boat in the area. When the United States entered the war, German submarine warfare was initially remarkably successful. From December 1941 to August 1942, 600 Allied ships were sunk crossing the Atlantic Ocean. Not until 1943, with the institution of the convoy system and improved air cover, did merchant ship losses finally begin to decline. By the end of the war, we know that German submarine losses were enormous. Of the 820 German submarines involved in the Battle of the Atlantic, 95 percent had been destroyed in action. Nevertheless, even as the war wound down, a few U-boats continued to lurk along the eastern coast of the United States.

One of these was *U-853*. The submarine was commanded by Helmut Froemsdorf, a twenty-four-year-old captain determined to carry out German grand admiral Karl Donitz's orders to sink as many Allied ships as possible before the war ended. "Above all, our honor demands that we fight to the end," Donitz cabled his commanders in March 1945. Captain Froemsdorf was unaware, however, that the German code had been broken in 1941 by British cryptographers.

United States intelligence experts were therefore aware of Donitz's communications. They had been tracking a German submarine in the Gulf of Maine throughout April and had issued an alert to all ships. The problem was that Berlin had no recent radio contact from the sub, so it was difficult to know exactly where the U-boat was located. In the meantime, two ships had been sunk off the coast of Nova Scotia.

Captain Froemsdorf spotted *Eagle 56* sitting dead in the water, a short distance away, at noon on April 23. To the U-boat captain and the fifty-five cramped and restless men on board, it was a dream come true. *U-853* had been forced to remain below the surface for most of the Atlantic crossing, and the crew was exhausted from evading Allied ships and aircraft that had already sunk more than one hundred U-boats in 1945. This was the moment they had been waiting for. Froemsdorf brought his ship to within six hundred yards of *Eagle 56* and gave the order to fire.

The blast blew the old sub chaser out of the water, breaking its keel and killing five of the six officers, including Commander James Early, and forty-four members of the crew. Lieutenant John Scagnelli was flung from his bunk and sustained a deep cut to his scalp, although he remained conscious, which probably saved his life. "I was thrown just as though someone had picked me up and tossed me," he said. The stern section of the ship sank almost immediately, although the bow remained afloat for fifteen minutes before it sank.

Scagnelli groped his way to the deck and jumped into the freezing water along with a handful of other sailors who had managed to get off the stricken ship. Scagnelli, a former college athlete, was a powerful swimmer, although only about half the men in the water were able to survive until relief vessels arrived. Six of the surviving thirteen men would later testify that they had seen a submarine.

The destroyer USS *Selfridge* arrived within twenty minutes and began to pull frozen sailors from the water. A few minutes later, SONAR contact was made with a submarine half a mile away. Almost immediately, the *Selfridge*'s captain got underway and ordered a depth charge attack. With rescue in sight, tragically, the destroyer's propellers sucked several more of the *Eagle 56*'s crew down to their deaths. "The captain had no choice," a member of the *Selfridge* crew would regretfully say later.

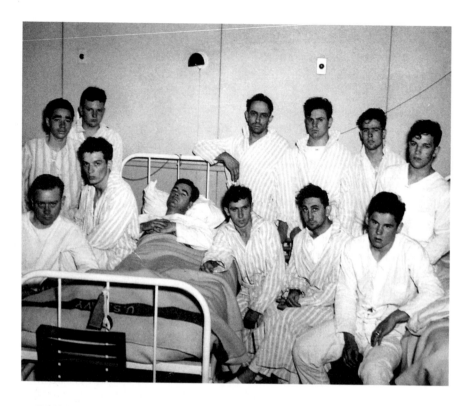

Selfridge dropped several depth charges to no avail and returned to pick up a total of twelve survivors. At the same time, the USS *Nantucket* arrived and plucked a lucky thirteenth survivor from the waters. At this point, no one was quite sure what had caused the explosion. Had USS *Eagle* hit a mine, or was it really a torpedo from a submarine? The *Portland Press Herald* called it "a mysterious boat blast."

U-853 continued to roam the waters of the mid-Atlantic coast until May 4, when Admiral Doenitz, who had replaced Hitler after his suicide, issued general orders to surrender. Apparently, Captain Froemsdorf never received the message. The following day, SS *Black Point* was carrying a load of coal along the Rhode Island coast en route to Boston when it was torpedoed within three miles of Point Judith Lighthouse. The ship sank within fifteen minutes, taking twelve members of the crew to their deaths.

A nearby freighter rescued thirty-four survivors and broadcast the alert. The area was almost immediately swarming with warships ready to prevent the sub from escaping. It was now known to be *U-853*. Shortly after sinking *Black Point*, the sub had briefly surfaced before it quickly dove. Fourteen warships immediately drew a net around the doomed submarine and began

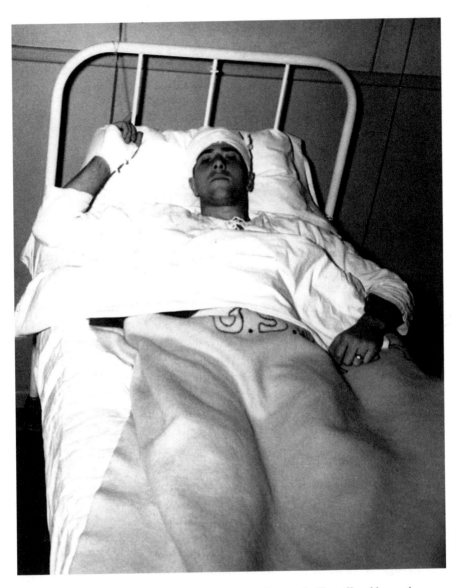

Above: John Scagnelli in his hospital bed following the attack. He suffered lacerations to his scalp and injured his wrist in addition to suffering from hypothermia. *Courtesy of Stephen Puleo.*

Opposite: Twelve of the "lucky thirteen" USS *Eagle 56* survivors shown in the hospital shortly after their rescue. *Courtesy of Stephen Puleo.*

a systematic SONAR search. In the shallow waters of Rhode Island Sound, it was only a matter of time before *U-853* was detected and destroyed by depth charges. Divers confirmed the U-boat's destruction in 130 feet of water on May 6.

The Court of Inquiry

Three days after *Eagle 56* was sunk, a Court of Inquiry was formed to investigate the circumstances of its sinking. Surviving members of the crew were interviewed, including John Scagnelli, who stated that the engines and boilers were in good condition and had recently been overhauled in Rockland. Scagnelli concluded his testimony feeling that he had persuaded the board that the explosion had not been caused by a faulty boiler.

Stephen Puleo devoted a chapter in *Due to Enemy Action* to the court's proceedings and included a transcript of the testimony of several crewmembers, at least two of whom stated that they saw a submarine. The decision was announced on May 2: "The only plausible conclusion that this court can logically reach is that the ship was destroyed by a catastrophic boiler explosion." Scagnelli and the remaining crewmembers were staggered.

Years later, Scagnelli would state:

> *They stacked the deck with that Court of Inquiry. It was an embarrassment to the Navy, allowing an enemy warship to get in so close…People would have asked, "Where were your surveillance ships?" Secondly, I think they didn't want people to know U-boats were still operating so close to our shores. Hell, people believed the war with Germany was almost over.*

Scagnelli also questioned whether there was an engineering officer on the board of inquiry. "If there was," he fumed, "he would have realized it would have taken ten boilers, all exploding at the same time, to do the damage that was done to our ship."

After recovering from his wound, John Scagnelli was transferred to Washington, D.C., and spent his final weeks in the navy writing condolence letters to relatives of crewmembers who had perished. He was ordered to make no mention of a torpedo attack or that the ship had halted. "The book was to be closed on the *Eagle 56* story," wrote Puleo. Failure to do this would have resulted in a court-martial for Scagnelli.

Paul Lawton's Quest

On a chilly March night in 1998, a thirty-eight-year-old lawyer named Paul Lawton was sitting in a bar in Brockton, Massachusetts, talking with his friends Bob and Paul Westerlund. Lawton, an avid scuba diver, was also an expert on U-boats and their role in the Battle of the Atlantic. When Bob Westerlund told him that a German sub had sunk his father's ship off the Maine coast in 1945, Lawton was shocked. He knew that *U-853* had sunk the collier *Black Point* shortly at the end of the war, but this was the first time he had heard that *Eagle 56* may also have been a victim. The navy had been clear about it: no U.S. warships had ever been sunk by U-boats in New England waters.

The Westerlund brothers also told Lawton that their mother never believed the official navy version of a faulty boiler. The lawyer/historian/diver immediately moved into action. "I just couldn't believe it," Lawton said. "Why would the navy say it was a boiler explosion?"

Back at his house, Lawton reexamined the World War II classic *Axis Submarine Successes, 1939–1945*, by Jurgen Rohwer. A reference caught his eye of a "probable" sinking of USS *Eagle* near Portland when *U-853* was in apparently the area. In an article written in 2003 called "Setting the Record Straight; Sinking of PE 56," historian Helen O'Neill picked up the story:

> *If indeed Eagle 56 had been sunk by an enemy submarine, the forty-nine men who died in the disaster would have been entitled to Purple Hearts. They were entitled to more than simply being written off as victims of a freak accident.*

Helen O'Neill continued, noting Lawton's involvement:

> *Lawton began combing through the archives, calling military historians, and writing letters to various branches of the Navy. He requested the report from the court of inquiry into the sinking, and also witness statements and deck logs. "Sorry," the replies came back, "the files were missing and presumed lost."*

After six months pursuing leads to no avail, Lawton told the Westerlunds that he was being stonewalled. Anxious to help their friend with the investigation, the Westerlund brothers placed a notice in the *Boston Globe* saying that they were looking for survivors of *Eagle 56*. Johnny

Breeze, a retired Boeing machinist, was visiting his daughter in Peabody, Massachusetts, in October 1998 when she showed him the notice and asked, "Dad, wasn't this your ship?" Breeze immediately called Paul Westerlund, who put him in touch with Paul Lawton.

In his conversations with Lawton, Breeze emphasized that the *Eagle 56* boilers were in good running order. Furthermore, Breeze confirmed that he and several other crewmen had seen a sub as they were leaving the sinking ship. "Hey Breeze," he remembered Oscar Davis saying, "there's a sub." "And I looked off the port quarter, and there was a sub."

Another person who saw the notice in the *Globe* was Alice Heyd Hultgren, a former WAVE and a stenographer at the board of inquiry in 1945. She also proved to be a valuable resource, since she had been present when each of the survivors gave his account. Hultgren told Lawton, "I remember more than one man saying that he thought it was a torpedo or a sub. One fellow said he had been on another ship that had been sunk and it felt like the same thing."

The testimonies of Breeze and Hultgren filled eighteen pages. Helen O'Neill wrote, "To Lawton it was clear that top Naval officials knew that the *Eagle* had been sunk by a German submarine. They just could not bring themselves to publicly admit it." Undeterred, the tenacious Lawton planned a dive to search for the remains of the sunken ship. "We hope an inspection of the wreckage will provide evidence of the true case of her [*Eagle 56*] loss, and may help rewrite this chapter of U.S. Naval history."

A dramatic breakthrough occurred in the fall of 1999 when, on her seventy-seventh birthday, Alice Hultgren received a package containing the lost testimony of the 1945 Court of Inquiry. The package was sent by an old friend, retired navy captain Edward Melanson, with whom she had discussed the case. Hultgren quickly contacted Paul Lawton, who immediately got in touch with other survivors who were listed in the court's testimony. One was Harold Peterson, who also confirmed that *Eagle*'s engines were "working beautifully."

Eighteen months passed as Lawton fruitlessly petitioned the navy to reopen the case. The matter finally ended up on the desk of Bernard Cavalcante at the Naval Historical Center early in 2001. The archivist was also familiar with the work of the German submarine historian Jurgen Rohwer. Helen O'Neill reported that "Cavalcante read Lawton's work in shock and was appalled by the Navy's response. He realized it was time to set the record straight."

Cavalcante sent a copy of Lawton's report to Secretary of the Navy Gordon England, stating that at least one of *Eagle 56*'s survivors had seen the

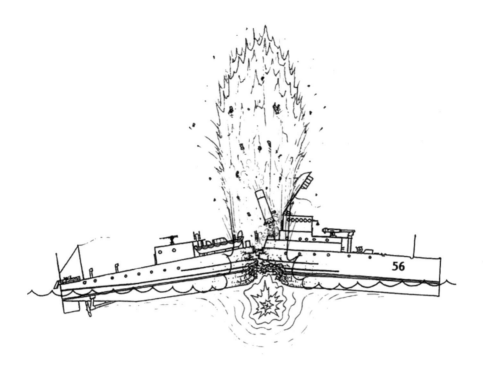

Lawyer Paul Lawton's drawing of the explosion that sank USS *Eagle 56* on Monday April 23, 1945. *Courtesy of Stephen Puleo.*

distinctive red trotting horse on a yellow shield marking on *U-853*'s conning tower. (This information had come from U-boat archives in Germany.) Because of this, the forty-nine *Eagle 56* crewmembers who had died should receive Purple Heart Medals.

More time passed by until, finally, in the summer of 2001, navy secretary Gordon England took the unusual step of reversing the decision made by the board of inquiry fifty-three years earlier. To partly justify the board's original decision, Cavalcante explained that "the Board did not have the intelligence information available and they had no way of knowing *U-853* was in the area. A colossal mess up? Yes. But a deliberate cover-up? No. I don't believe so."

Thousands of people across the nation, including eighty-one-year-old John Scagnelli living in Morris Plains, New Jersey, read newspaper stories of the navy reversing the board of inquiry's decision. According to Stephen Puleo, Scagnelli "had put the events of April 23, 1945 behind him, but never beyond the reach of his memories." Since returning to civilian life,

Scagnelli had spent his life as a social worker, helping people less fortunate than himself. The former naval officer told Puleo that the events of April 23, 1945, "helped me determined what my future was going to be."

On the morning of June 8, 2002, a solemn ceremony was held aboard USS *Salem* in Quincy Bay, Massachusetts. As the surviving officer, John Scagnelli had the honor of reading the names of those who died "due to enemy action" and would receive the Purple Heart. The medal was awarded posthumously to those survivors who had died since 1945.

At the end of the ceremony, the three survivors present—John Scagnelli, Johnny Breeze and Harold Peterson—stepped forward and presented Paul Lawton with a cherry wood plaque. The inscription expressed their gratitude to Lawton for his incredibly tenacious four-year quest and concluded with the words, "We thank you from the bottom of our hearts."

Note: As of this writing, the submerged wreck of PE 56 has not been found.

Part II

The Urban Flotilla

CITY OF RICHMOND GETS LOST IN THE FOG

Shortly after the Civil War, an elegant coastal steamer was built in Athens, New York, at the Norton and Edmunds boatyard. Athens is a historic little village on the Hudson River, halfway between New York City and Albany, New York. Because of its location on the river, Athens has had a long shipbuilding tradition.

Settlers appeared in the late seventeenth century, and Athens soon became a convenient point from which to cross the river. A local man, Conrad Flaack, was one of the first to start a ferry business in 1778, using a canoe to carry passengers and two boats with a platform laid across to carry carriages. Steam vessels appeared in the early nineteenth century, and by the 1830s, Athens was thriving, with barges, sailing ships and steamboats carrying on active trade in brickmaking, shipbuilding and ice harvesting.

At first, most traders built their own vessels, but by the 1850s, William Morton and Emery Edwards had formed a shipbuilding business. Several steam screw ships were built in the early 1860s, and in 1865, the partners launched their prize vessel, the side-wheeler *City of Richmond*.

City of Richmond was built for the Baltimore Steam Packet Company, also known as the Old Bay Line, for service on the Chesapeake Bay following

City of Richmond was called the "most graceful in appearance of all the side wheel steamers that plied the waters of Penobscot Bay." *From the collections of Maine Historical Society/Maine Memory Network.*

the Civil War. The company's hopes of resuming business with southern markets was premature, however, and after a year, *City of Richmond* was purchased by the Portland, Bangor and Machias Steamboat Company for use in Maine.

With a 350-horsepower engine, the swift 227-foot-long steamer soon became the flagship of the line. (It also sported the first chime whistle to be heard on the Maine coast.) *City of Richmond*'s speed was initially challenged by another Hudson River–built boat, *Milton Martin*, ironically referred to as "a stranger from the Hudson." After "an unproductive year" of trying to keep up with *Richmond* on the Portland-Bangor run, the outclassed *Milton Martin* was returned to the Hudson River route. For the remainder of the 1870s, *City of Richmond* was used on a variety of New England routes and commanded by several different captains.

The Wreck

The *Rockland Courier Gazette* called *City of Richmond* "[t]he most graceful in appearance of all the side wheel steamers that once plied the waters of

Penobscot Bay." Unfortunately, it was the great speed of *City of Richmond* that caused the ship to run onto Robinson Rock at the southern tip of the Islesboro chain of islands in West Penobscot Bay.

City of Richmond left Portland Harbor on August 29, 1881, for the first of its three weekly round trips to Bar Harbor on Mount Desert. The ship completed "a delightful run" to Rockland, the weather being "clear and fine." The next morning, however, the area was blanketed by thick fog. Rather than follow its normal route from Rockland through a narrow channel of the Fox Islands Thorofare (between Vinalhaven and North Haven) to Mount Desert, *Richmond*'s captain, William E. Dennison, charted a northeasterly course. This would take the vessel diagonally across Penobscot Bay and around the north end of North Haven Island.

City of Richmond left Tilson's Wharf in Rockland at 6:00 a.m. on August 30. The ship sped through the fog for eight miles, with the watch keeping a sharp lookout. Twenty minutes later, Captain Dennison was chilled by the sound of the ship's foghorn echoing off the shore of a nearby island. Dennison immediately changed course, thinking that he was still a safe distance from the ledge just south of Mark Island.

Suddenly, a spindle (a marker) loomed up off the port bow. Before Captain Dennison could slow the engines, the 875-ton vessel ran hard on Robinson Rock, below Mark Island. In a minute, the steamer's bow was perched high on the rocks, making a hole in the hull through which water was pouring rapidly. The next day, the *Rockland Courier Gazette* announced, "*Richmond* lies between the spindle on the inner end and the buoy on the outer end of the ledge [Robinson Rock]. A hundred feet or less southwest would have carrier her clear."

According to a September 2, 1881 account from the *Maine Industrial Journal*, "The captain and officers acquitted themselves with great credit and no panic ensued." The *Rockland Free Press* added, "Captain Dennison was very pale, but calm and efficient as ever. The officers were perfectly cool and immediately took measures to boat the passengers ashore."

All sixty passengers were landed safely on uninhabited Mark Island about one hundred yards away. Breakfast had been prepared before the accident, and amazingly, hot coffee and such food as could be found were immediately sent ashore. All the baggage and most of the freight were also saved, as well as "such movables" that could be reached in the brief time allowed.

The hull of *City of Richmond* filled rapidly with water as it sat on Robinson Rock. The ship's staterooms and upper works had broken away and were cut loose to ease the strain on the hull.

City of Richmond ran on Robinson Rock on September 2, 1881. Passengers were landed safely on Mark Island, seen on the right-hand side of the picture. *Author's collection.*

A messenger was dispatched to Camden from whence the little steamer *Planet* was sent to pick up passengers and deliver them to Rockland. The *Pioneer* and *Henry Morgan* from the Vinalhaven line also appeared to help ferry passengers, as well as to remove bedding and other furniture that could be saved from the wreck. Oliver Lovejoy, deck boy on *Henry Morgan*, related that the crew and some of the officers remained with the ship throughout the day, trying to save what they could.

The next day, W.F. Milliken, president of the Portland, Bangor and Machias line, appeared on another company steamer, *Lewiston*, to inspect the damage. The salvage experts who accompanied him told Milliken that all hopes of saving the steamer should be abandoned and that preparations should be made to hoist the machinery out of the stricken vessel.

The *Rockland Free Press* reported, "Thus we have probably seen the last of the good steamer *City of Richmond*. She was a great favorite, being very speedy and always fortunate by having able and courteous officers." The paper was careful not to blame Captain Dennison or his pilot directly, but its reporter was clearly not satisfied with the explanations of what had caused the accident:

> *The officers have been long on duty and have run the line with remarkable safety. These are facts which will prevent hasty censure, but they cannot be safely allowed to prevent such rigid inquiry as shall impress upon public carriers their responsibility and accountability.*

The previous year, *City of Richmond* and its sister ship, *Lewiston*, had been elegantly refurbished at a cost of $30,000. There was a fire insurance policy but no marine insurance on either vessel. The *Maine Industrial Journal* sadly reported, "Richmond was not insured and the loss will be about $50,000."

The *Industrial Journal* then gave a vote of confidence to Dennison and his beleaguered pilot:

> *Persons unfamiliar with the rock bound shores of our State have no conception of the obstacles which have to be overcome by the brave commanders and efficient officers who have charge of the steamers in Maine waters. This steamboat casualty is not a surprise. It is more to be wondered that the record of steam boating in our waters is so free from disasters. Captain Dennison and his first-pilot Pollister have no superiors in Maine steamboat circles.*

A New Life

After six attempts, *City of Richmond* was refloated and towed to Portland for an overhaul. It remained in service for another twenty years. *Courtesy of Library of Congress, Prints and Photographs Division.*

City of Richmond was down but not out. A few days later, a reporter from the *Rockland Courier Gazette* visited the scene of the disaster and was told by the company general manager Cushing that the steamer was in better shape than had originally been feared. After six attempts, the venerable vessel was finally refloated and taken to the South

Marine Railway pier in Rockland for patching up. From there, the ship was towed to Portland to be overhauled.

When the Maine Central Railroad purchased the Portland, Bangor and Machias Steamboat Company in 1882, the newly rebuilt *City of Richmond* was transferred to the Mount Desert and Machiasport run. Captain Dennison continued to command his ship until 1892, when the old craft was replaced by a new steamer, *Frank Jones*.

From Maine, *City of Richmond* was sold to business interests in New London, Connecticut, where it was briefly operated as an excursion boat. A few years later, *Richmond* headed south, where the vessel was renamed *City of Key West* and used in the Spanish-American War. According to an article in *Down East* magazine by Allie Ryan, the craft Mainers knew as *City of Richmond* spent its final days as a houseboat in Perth Amboy, New Jersey.

THE "TREASURE" SHIP: SS *CAMBRIDGE*

Every shipwreck has its particular set of characteristics. Some vessels are destroyed in violent storms. Others lose their bearings in the fog and run on the rocks, and some are consumed by fire. What was unusual about the SS

SS *Cambridge* was built in 1867 and was originally commanded by Captain Charles Sanford, founder and owner of the Sanford Independent Line. *Courtesy of John Flint.*

Cambridge disaster was that the ship's cargo, valued at $200,000, was scattered in a wide area around Old Man Ledge, which is five miles from Port Clyde. As a result, for more than 125 years, the wreck has attracted divers. The search has slowed in the twenty-first century, although there is still the occasional diver who hunts for artifacts scattered around the ledge.

The Accident

The steamer *Cambridge* left Boston on a calm evening carrying forty passengers and a load of freight on February 9, 1886. The sea was "as smooth as a puddle," according to a newspaper account, as the ship proceeded on its four-times-per-week run up the coast to Bangor. Under the command of famed captain Otis Ingraham, the pride of the Boston and Bangor Steamship Company sped through the chilly night at twelve knots per hour.

Old Man Ledge is a modest-sized chunk of jagged granite that is barely covered by water at low tide. It was marked by a can buoy, five miles off the coast, and sits midway between Port Clyde and Monhegan Island. Captain Ingraham had left the bridge at 3:00 a.m. and turned command of the ship over to First Pilot William Rodgers. Suddenly, at 4:45 a.m., SS *Cambridge* ran hard on the ledge. The vessel heeled sharply to starboard, and with an ebbing tide, there was little doubt that the craft was there to stay.

Pilot William Rodgers never was able to satisfactorily explain why *Cambridge* ran on the rocks. Perhaps, on a bitterly cold night, the bow watchman William Jacobs was more concerned with staying warm than keeping his eyes peeled for the can buoy. (He later offered the dubious excuse that the buoy was so covered with snow that he thought it was a floating cake of ice.) Or perhaps, at a critical point, the helmsman applied too much left rudder. Or perhaps Rogers was still brooding over his failure to be given command of *Cambridge*. The moody pilot had hoped that he would be chosen when, instead, the directors of the Boston and Bangor Company, formerly known as the Sanford Independent Line, gave the position to Otis Ingraham.

The bottom line, however, was that for a sailor with twenty-four years' experience on this particular run, William Rodgers should have been more aware of the ship's location. (His grandson would later blame sea smoke for limiting his visibility.) Another theory for the accident was that an onshore wind and incoming tide had driven *Cambridge* much closer to the mainland than Rodgers realized. (*Cambridge* was nearly one mile off course when the accident occurred.) Not surprisingly, the wreck ended the career of William

A painting of *Cambridge* passing through the North Haven Thorofare. The Camden Hills are seen in the background. *Courtesy of John Flint.*

Rodgers, although in the ensuing Court of Inquiry, he was never officially blamed for the disaster.

SS *Cambridge* was built at a cost of $250,000 in 1867. With a three-hundred-horsepower engine, the swift vessel quickly became the flagship of the Boston and Bangor Company. Cambridge was 248 feet long with a 37-foot beam and drew 12 feet. It was the first steamer east of Cape Cod to have a dining room on the saloon deck, which made it a passenger favorite, especially with the ladies. John Richardson in *Steamboats of the Penobscot* called it "the first of the local moderns."

The *Rockland Courier Gazette* referred to *Cambridge* as "a smart steamer and one of the fastest side wheelers ever to operate in [down] Eastern waters." Many times, *Cambridge* would arrive in Bangor after its overnight run from Boston before its sister ship, *Katahdin*, was ready to leave the dock for the trip south.

Cambridge had the additional advantage of having Rockland's Otis Ingraham, commodore of the Sanford Steamship fleet, as its captain. William Rodgers notwithstanding, Ingraham had earned the right to command the ship when, on more than one occasion, he had saved the vessel from destruction.

Ingraham was the ship's first mate when *Cambridge* struck a rock near Monhegan Island in 1869. The vessel was filling with water when the intrepid Ingraham launched a lifeboat and saved the ship by fastening a heavy tarpaulin over the stove-in section of the hull. With the pumps working furiously, *Cambridge* limped into Rockland, where it was repaired.

Ingraham was also first officer when *Cambridge* was caught in a nasty September storm, curiously also near Monhegan. A huge wave knocked out the rudder and broke off the steam pipe, causing the ship to drift helplessly toward the New Harbor ledges. As the ship neared the shallow waters off the rocky coast, Ingraham ordered both anchors let go. Everyone held their breath until the ship came to a stop. Thanks to Ingraham's clever move, *Cambridge* was saved again.

Unfortunately, there was no saving *Cambridge* when it hit Old Man Ledge early on the morning of February 10, 1886. First Engineer William Fox described the scene: "Several pipes

Top: A poster advertising the schedules of *Cambridge* and its sister ship, *Kathadin*, in 1881. *Courtesy of John Flint.*

Left: *Cambridge*'s Captain Otis Ingraham was the senior captain in the Boston and Bangor Company fleet and one of the most colorful figures in Penobscot Bay's steamboat history. *Author's collection.*

burst when the steamer struck and steam began to escape from all sides." Fox stayed at his post, ably assisted by Second Engineer Larry Flynn, until all the steam had escaped and a disaster from steam and fire was averted.

Captain Ingraham had immediately come on deck. Cool and decisive as ever, he quickly ordered the boats to be launched. The forty passengers, women and children first, were loaded into six lifeboats and rowed by the crew to safety on nearby Allen Island. There they were sheltered in a fisherman's house. No one was injured or even got wet.

The Rescue

At dawn the next morning, a young man named Maloney, living on Pleasant Point Road in Cushing, looked down the St. George River and saw what he thought was a wrecked ship on the rocks beyond the Georges Islands at the mouth of the river. We don't know Maloney's first name, but the young man grabbed a spyglass and was able to distinguish the outlines of a disabled steamer.

Maloney jumped on his horse and rode to Thomaston, where he told the story to Dr. H.C. Levensaler, a correspondent for the *Rockland Courier Gazette*. Levensaler telegraphed the newspaper office in Rockland inquiring if the steamer *Cambridge* had made a stop in Rockland, which, of course, it had not. This was the first inkling that there had been a disaster, and the word quickly spread.

In Rockland, the revenue cutter *Dallas*, under the command of Captain Barr, was about to begin its daily run from Rockland to Portland. When he heard the news, Barr immediately headed for Allen Island, accompanied by other rescue vessels from Rockland. The armada arrived at about 9:00 a.m., and Barr supervised the safe transfer of passengers and most of the crew and headed back to Rockland. The fleet of rescue ships arrived at Tilson's Wharf at noon on February 10, with *Dallas* sounding its whistle to celebrate the successful rescue. A sympathetic crowd soon gathered to welcome the weary travelers.

The passengers were treated like celebrities and taken to the Thorndike Hotel, where they were lodged overnight at the company's expense. The next day, a steamer arrived to take them on to Bangor. The passengers were effusive in their praise for the actions of Captain Barr and his crew and adopted the following resolution as reported in the *Rockland Courier-Gazette*:

> *The passengers of the wrecked steamer Cambridge desire to express to Commander Barr, his officers and crew of the revenue cutter Dallas, their*

grateful acknowledgments for the prompt assistance and generous attention received at their hands.

One passenger, E. Dudley Freeman from Yarmouth, later wrote to the *Portland Press* and severely criticized the crew of SS *Cambridge*, saying that "they knew nothing about clearing away the lifeboats." It should be noted that the disgruntled Mr. Freeman was the only one of the forty passengers who did not speak highly of the behavior of the officers and crew. Other passengers stated that the crew acted "nobly, leaving their berths as soon as the alarm was sounded and going calmly and coolly to their posts of duty."

The Search for Valuables

About two-thirds of the passengers' personal luggage was saved from the ship, but nearly everything else on SS *Cambridge* was lost, which brings us to the next phase of the story. When it hit Old Man Ledge, *Cambridge* was literally broken in two and sank within two hours. Thanks to Captain Ingraham's cool head, however, everyone got off the ship before the hull disappeared beneath the waves.

W.B. Eaton, *Cambridge*'s purser, described the ship's cargo as "[o]ne of the largest and most valuable freights ever put on board." As was the case in all shipwrecks, once word of the disaster spread, the area was swarming with fishing boats from Port Clyde, Friendship, Tenants Harbor, Monhegan and elsewhere, all looking for portions of the freight as it washed out of the hold.

Admiralty, or maritime law, is complicated, although practically speaking, it is "everyone for himself." In legal terms, "when property is lost at sea and rescued by another, the rescuer is entitled to claim a salvage award on the saved property." Knowing this, Captain Ingraham, accompanied by several loyal crewmembers, remained in a lifeboat near the wreck for hours in an attempt to protect the cargo from being looted by local residents. When the exhausted Ingraham was finally forced to head for Rockland, the scavengers closed in.

John Flint is a retired sea captain and a resident of Cushing, Maine. A number of years ago, Flint was preparing a lecture series on Maine shipwrecks when his friend John Olson, a Cushing lobsterman, told him about the *Cambridge* disaster on Old Man Ledge. Flint naturally was interested and went out in Olson's boat to dive and photograph the area around the site of the wreck.

Above: This stake was put on Old Man Ledge to mark the rocks that *Cambridge* hit in 1886. The bent shaft shows the effects of a severe winter storm. *Courtesy of John Flint.*

Opposite: A sketch of the *Cambridge* debris field, drawn by John Flint in 1983. *Courtesy of John Flint.*

Captain Flint told me that "the water was clear and that his diving team spotted the anchors almost immediately as well as the anchor capstan standing upright on the ocean floor." Not surprisingly, except for a few pieces of ironwork, everything else had long ago been washed away by the sea surge or taken by divers.

In his lecture on the wreck of *Cambridge* at the Penobscot Marine Museum, Flint described what happened once Captain Ingraham and his crewmen departed:

> For the next twenty-four hours, the natives were out in force and anything that was not nailed down was removed by enterprising coastal residents. Doors, hardware, carpeting and metal work were all "transferred" to local homes…
>
> The keeper of the Franklin Island Light headed over in his dory and with a hacksaw removed a quantity of brass and copper pipe. He returned with a full load, landed his take on the beach and decided to return for a

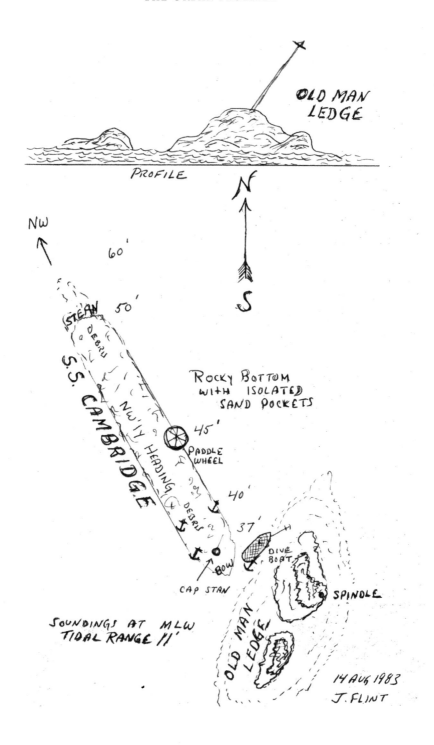

PROFILE

OLD MAN LEDGE

N

S

NW

60'

50'

STERN

DEBRIS

S.S. CAMBRIDGE

NW'ly HEADING

DEBRIS

ROCKY BOTTOM
WITH ISOLATED
SAND POCKETS

45'

PADDLE
WHEEL

40'

37'

DIVE
BOAT

BOW

CAP STAN

SPINDLE

OLD MAN LEDGE

SOUNDINGS AT MLW
TIDAL RANGE 11'

14 AUG 1983
J. FLINT

second load. He was too late, the ship had gone down. When he returned to the beach he discovered that an enterprising soul had neatly filched all the pipe he had so laboriously collected.

Old Cap Simmons from Friendship had boarded Cambridge and scooped up all the silverware from the dining saloon. I guess someone didn't like Simmons because they informed the sheriff. Simmons had friends, however, who advised him of the lawman's impending visit and he carefully buried the silverware under his woodpile and so indeed he had the last laugh.

Flint also told the story of the time he was invited to visit Betsy Wyeth at her island home near the site of the wreck. "I want you to see something I don't understand," she told him as he was being showed around the house. In the bedroom, she pointed to a lopsided headboard on her bed. Flint asked her if it came from the area. Betsy then told him it was one of the doors from the looted *Cambridge*. Flint told her that the doors on ships are not square and that, years ago, someone had taken the panels from one of the steamer's doors and made a headboard for a bed.

The *Belfast American* also described the search for valuables by American Empress Company agent Weeks in the months that followed. Weeks located the company's trunk containing twenty-six packages being held by Captain William Condon, who lived in Friendship. After prolonged negotiations, Condon refused to give up his salvage, and Weeks turned the matter over to local authorities.

Weeks found the piano from *Cambridge*'s saloon in a Monhegan Island house in a somewhat damaged condition but still playable. (How it was transported to Monhegan was not clear.) Weeks did say, "The natives by use of main strength can execute difficult music upon it." As a result, Weeks decided to leave the instrument where it was. Another piano was not so fortunate. A man from Friendship found it floating in the water, but it was so badly damaged that it could not be used.

A group of eastern Maine merchants who also had cargo on *Cambridge* belatedly visited the scene of the wreck hoping to recover some of their goods. The steamer *Henry Morrison* was chartered to help them locate lost freight, although the expedition was generally unsuccessful. The bulk of their goods had sunk with the ship or had been seized by enterprising fishermen.

At one point, *Henry Morrison* stopped at Monhegan, where some of the inhabitants proudly, but naïvely, displayed the articles they had salvaged. The residents were described in a news report as "very honorable in their dealings," and several of the merchants were able to retrieve a number of lost items.

Probably the most important piece of salvage was *Cambridge*'s two thirty-five-ton boilers, which had recently been reconditioned. Fortunately, divers hired by the International Steamship Company were able to raise them. When they were found to be in good condition, the company owners purchased the boilers and had them installed in the steamer *New York*, which was undergoing an extensive refit in Portland.

For the next six months, divers searched the area around Old Man Ledge, where the remains of the steamer *Cambridge* lay. Nothing else of importance was found other than the paddle wheels and a few pieces of debris. The *Maine Industrial Journal* noted:

> *The tide runs very strong around the ledge and it was not unfrequent* [sic] *for the toiler* [diver] *beneath the waves to be picked up and carried twenty feet by the force of the sea. Portions of the ship's upper works and other floatable wreckage were eventually scattered along the coast from White Head to Kittery.*

Epilogue

At the conclusion of his lecture, Captain John Flint provided his audience with a not-so-subtle criticism of Pilot William Rogers's actions in regard to the wreck of SS *Cambridge*:

> *Nothing in these rules shall exonerate any vessel or the owner, master or crew thereof, from the consequences of any neglect to carry lights or signals or neglect to keep a proper lookout or precaution which may be required by the ordinary practice of seamen or by the special circumstances of the case.*

AN ACCIDENT-PRONE SHIP: *CITY OF ROCKLAND*

City of Rockland was the elegant flagship of the Eastern Steamship Company, yet its twenty-three years of operation were marred by frequent disasters. These began in 1903 when the ship crashed into the slip of the Boston, Revere Beach and Lynn Railroad ferry. Little damage was done to the steamer, although there was some destruction to the property of the railroad company. The following year, however, a serious accident occurred in the southwest corner of Penobscot Bay. In retrospect, these events set the tone for the career of the popular ship.

Two years later, in 1906, the vessel collided with its sister ship, *City of Bangor*, off Portland. A few years later, *City of Rockland*'s bow was smashed in, and it was beached following a collision near Boone Island in southern Maine. The accident-prone ship suffered several more mishaps while on the Boston–Kennebec River route before running on a ledge off Parker's Head at the mouth of the Kennebec River in September 1923. After the three hundred passengers were unloaded, *City of Rockland* was refloated and towed to Boston. Following a survey, it was decided that repairs were impossible, and the ship was condemned. A year later, *City of Rockland* was towed to Little Misery Island off of Salem, Massachusetts, and burned on October 29, 1924.

The Ship

City of Rockland was a wooden steamer that was built at a cost of $350,000 by William McKie in his east Boston yard in 1900. At the time of its launching, it was the largest side-wheel steamer ship in New England waters, as it was almost three hundred feet long. *City of Rockland* had a gross tonnage of 1,700 and was powered by two 1,700-horsepower engines. The ship had two hundred staterooms and could carry four hundred passengers. A report in the *Rockland Opinion* described the vessel as "not only a popular craft, but a flyer." The ship had a top speed of twenty-one knots under optimal conditions.

City of Rockland joined the Eastern Steamship Company fleet in 1901 and made its maiden voyage from Boston to Bangor in June of that year. The ship made stops at Camden, Belfast, Searsport, Bucksport and Winterport. At each town, selected visitors were invited to go on board, view the interior of the steamer and continue as guests of the company for the remainder of the trip. In Bangor, an evening reception was planned with music and refreshments.

The *Bangor Commercial* noted:

> *Up in the pilothouse everyone is delighted, as they like the way the boat stands up and the way she keeps her course. She will be a better sea boat, they say, than the City of Bangor, as her hull is built on lines that were newly drawn for sea-going side-wheelers.*

City of Rockland seen crossing Penobscot Bay. The graceful steamship was described as "the Magnificent White Flyer, Queen of the Eastern Steamship Company." *Courtesy of Vinalhaven Historical Society.*

Her owners are surprised by the speed and ease with which she travels. It isn't often, the engineers say, that the stiffness is worked from the joints of an engine, the way they are coming from the powerful machines on the Rockland. It is a source of delight to the officers the way she minds her helm.

An Encounter with Upper Gangway Ledge

On a pleasant late July afternoon in 1904, *City of Rockland* left Boston, heading for Penobscot Bay under the command of Captain Marcus Pierce, a thirty-five-year veteran of the company. With four hundred passengers, a crew of one hundred and a full load of freight, newspapers described the graceful steamship as the "Magnificent White Flyer, Queen of the Eastern Steamship Company."

The vessel left Boston on schedule at 5:00 p.m. on July 25. Purser Robert Coombs noted, "When I retired at 10:00 pm the sky was clear as a bell, the moon was shining and there was not a ripple in the water. It was a most beautiful night." The situation would change rapidly in the next few hours.

Early in the morning of July 26, *City of Rockland* ran into a thick fog, which got worse as the steamer proceeded up the coast. In an interview with the *Rockland Star*, sixty-three-year-old Captain Pierce commented, "It was one of the thickest nights I have seen on this coast during my thirty-odd years of steam boating." Pierce added that they spent more than two hours in the vicinity of Monhegan getting their bearings and trying to pick up the whistling buoy off that island. When they finally located it, the pilot fixed a course for Whitehead Island and Spruce Head Island, which would take them to the Muscle Ridge Channel and hence to Rockland.

At about 5:20 a.m. on July 26, *City of Rockland* was groping its way through the Muscle Ridge Channel in a fog so thick that one passenger stated he could not see across the ship. Captain Pierce reduced the ship's speed to four knots when it ran on Upper Gangway Ledge with a "terrific crash." The impact broke the main steam pipe, disabling the ship's machinery, including the pumps, which were unable to clear the seawater pouring into the hull.

There are two Gangway Ledges in Muscle Ridge Channel, one at either end. They are so-called because they sit "right in the gangway" or in the middle of the thoroughfare. *City of Rockland* had passed Lower Gangway Ledge off Whitehead Island and was on course for the buoy can off Ash Island, leaving Upper Gangway Ledge to starboard, when the accident occurred. There is deep water on both sides of this ledge, but even a slight deviation from the course would result in running on the spread of rocks that extended out from Ash Island or hitting the Upper Gangway Ledge.

Perhaps to make up for lost time, *City of Rockland*'s pilot had chosen to take the narrow passage between Ash Island and Upper Gangway Ledge. In the thick early morning fog, the can buoy marking the ledge was difficult to pick out. Mariners agreed that this was, and still is, a very difficult channel for such a large ship to proceed through, even at four knots. The *Rockland Opinion* commented, "Hundreds of vessels have been wrecked along this section of the coast." The paper dryly opined, "The pilot of *City of Rockland* evidently believed he was well inside of Gangway Ledge when clearly he was not."

When *City of Rockland* hit Gangway Ledge, Captain Pierce immediately gave the order to stop the engines. "I would never back off a ledge not knowing where I was or how much water I was going into, for the vessel

The Rockland Daily Star.

ALL THE LOCAL NEWS AND ASSOCIATED PRESS SERVICE.

COLUMN XI, NO. 101.   ROCKLAND, ME., WEDNESDAY MORNING, JULY 27, 1904.   PRICE TWO CENTS

THE CITY OF ROCKLAND A WRECK

Queen Of Eastern Steamship Company's Fleet Ashore On Southwest Ledges And Probably A Total Loss

Struck At 5.30 O'clock Tuesday Morning On Gangway Ledge, And With Engines Disabled, Slid Off And Drifted At Mercy Of The Sea For Nearly Two Hours

City of Rockland's accident made the headlines in the local press. *Courtesy of Rockland Public Library.*

might have large holes in it and sink before the passengers could be landed," he said later. It turned out that *City of Rockland* was badly damaged on the starboard side, where a large hole of sixty by twenty feet had been opened up in the forward section of the ship.

The *Belfast Republican Journal* reported that when the steamer struck, it buckled in the middle and, as previously noted, the steam pipe broke. In an attempt to turn off the steam, the assistant engineer was scalded on his face and hands by escaping steam. Otherwise, no passenger or crewmember was seriously injured in the accident.

Captain Marcus Pierce then gave orders for the ship's whistle to be sounded repeatedly to notify those on shore of the accident. Hearing the whistle, the steamer *J. T. Morse*, which was sitting in Rockland Harbor seven miles away, headed immediately for the site of the disaster. Captain Pierce next lowered a boat and sent Second Mate George Williams to nearby Crescent Beach with instructions to telephone the company agent Raphael Sherman in Rockland for help.

Meanwhile, the rising tide had lifted *City of Rockland*, which was now filling with water, off Upper Gangway Ledge. Remarkably, the sinking ship proceeded to drift nearly two miles up the Muscle Ridge Channel, where it lodged on the Grindstone Ledges between Sheep and Fisherman's Islands. On board the ship, order was maintained; passengers donned life jackets, and six lifeboats and several life rafts were readied. Many passengers went to the baggage office to collect their belongings as they waited for rescue vessels to arrive.

Had *City of Rockland* not run on the Grindstone Ledges, the vessel would have undoubtedly sunk, with disastrous consequences for the hundreds of passengers and crew. Indeed, the *Rockland Opinion* observed that it was a miracle that the ship survived:

> *Here is a boat hard and fast on a ledge with the bottom ripped out of her. The tide floats her off full of water and just as she is sinking, lands her on about the only piece of rock in that part of Penobscot Bay that would hold her up out of water.*

As *City of Rockland* sank lower and lower, Captain Pierce gave orders for women and children to board the lifeboats. These quickly filled and headed for nearby Ash Island, guided through the fog by a local fisherman who fortuitously appeared in his dory. About 150 women and children were thus transported to Ash Island, where they would stay for most of the day. The rest of the passengers remained on board, hoping to be rescued by one of the larger vessels coming from Rockland.

Two hours after the accident, the steamer *J.T. Morse* finally appeared, having had trouble locating *City of Rockland* in the fog, and shortly afterward, the little mail boat *Catherine* showed up. By this time, *City of Rockland*'s deck was awash. Needless to say, the passengers (mostly men) who had remained on board were anxious to get off as soon as possible.

The decks of both rescue ships were soon crowded with people, some clutching their hand luggage, although their trunks remained below. There were four valuable horses in the hold, each worth more than $1,000. Although efforts were made to save the animals, the freight had shifted when the steamer struck so that the stalls were blocked, and they could not be rescued. The freight clerk's manifest showed that two belonged to Dr. Jackson from Searsport, and two were owned by a woman going to Bar Harbor.

When he was informed about the accident, Rockland agent Raphael Sherman quickly chartered tugs, sailboats and launches to remove all possible freight, movable articles and furnishing from *City of Rockland* while the ship was still afloat. An immense quantity of goods was thus removed and spread out on Newton's wharf in Rockland. Meanwhile, numerous other boats began to gather around the wreck, scavenging everything in sight.

Wreck Stories

A reporter from the *Lewiston Journal* was a member of the armada of boats surrounding the steamer. He described the scene as local fishermen jousted with one another to secure valuable pieces of wreckage:

The first sight of wreckage we passed was a cucumber. Then we passed a dead horse. Then we leaned over the side and drew in a nice fat cantaloupe. Then we passed a boy steering a catboat towing a barrel of flour. And then out of the haze and dispelling fog came the white sails of all sorts of craft, taking advantage of the spanking breeze and clearing weather to make port with the salvage of the wreck.

One craft was piled high with bedsteads, springs and mattresses. A gasoline launch went puffing into town with watermelons spread across her deck and the crew burying their noses in the rind. Another chap seems to have made a specialty of cabin windows, and another had the finest collection of crockery that you ever saw. I might enumerate the unusual picturesqueness of this down east Armada but it would take too long.

In Rockland, there was considerable agitation at the Eastern Steamship Company office, where company agent Sherman was trying to calm the crowd. When Sherman disembarked from a tug after visiting the wreck, he was besieged by men, many of whom were husbands who had last seen their wives and children heading for Ash Island in lifeboats. Eventually, all were reunited. The *Rockland Star* noted that "telephone and telegraph wires were hot with messages to all parts of the country telling friends or family of their safety and there was much hugging and kissing."

The Eastern Steamship Company's Rockland agent Sherman then chartered the steamer *Merryconeag* to take about two hundred of the stranded passengers to their destinations farther up the bay. The *Bangor Daily Commercial* interviewed a number of people about their experiences. One woman bound for Aroostook County had this to say:

I was awakened about 5:30 Tuesday morning by a terrible jar. I thought something had happened but an officer came to my stateroom and said it was caused by the boat striking the wharf at Rockland. I soon found out this was not true. Eventually I got to Rockland and left there for Bangor in the late afternoon.

A man who lost his luggage told a reporter:

I really though we had reached Rockland when we struck the ledge. An officer told me what happened, but that there was no immediate danger. We soon slid off the ledge and began to drift, when I noticed the steamer had settled considerably and begun to list. We were pretty scared when the boat hit the second ledge. It seemed a long time before the steamer from Rockland came to our rescue.

Mr. Fessenden was traveling with his wife from New York and described himself as "lucky to have the clothes on his back":

I had arisen at 5:00 and looked out the window when I noticed the can buoy come up out of the fog. Then we struck. It wasn't a sharp blow but a grating, tearing collision. Word was passed that the ship had run on a ledge but there was no excitement. The next word was that my wife and I should put on life preservers. I confess I felt apprehensive and nervous and as the time passed my apprehension increased.

In the meantime City of Rockland was sinking. There was no doubt about this. It is true the ship came off Gangway Ledges and drifted across bay and landed on the only rock in Penobscot Bay that would hold her. Providence seems to have had a good deal more to do with this than human reckoning.

The *Rockland Daily Star* described the initial reaction of the imperious Hortense Estes from Boston, who bemoaned the fact that she had lost the Worth gown that she was intending to wear at a Bar Harbor reception that evening:

Excited: Why certainly not! I love excitement but there was not enough to make one's blood tingle. I was dressing and, feeling the boat stop, I inquired the cause…I was dreadfully hungry and went in search of something to eat and was so disappointed that there was nothing.

The *Star* also reported that "there was a gentleman who had a big auto car in the hold bound for Bangor and was asking everyone if they couldn't help him to get it out. People had no time for autos just then and one cynical passenger told him to 'get up steam and ride ashore.'"

Then there was the lady from New York who implored the crew to save her trunk containing $16,000 worth of lace, while another woman claimed that she had a trunk full of jewelry worth $1,500 that was still in the hold.

One story in the *Bangor Daily Commercial* was headlined, "ALL LAUD PIERCE":

Rockland's passengers have the highest praise for the conduct of Captain Marcus Pierce and the members of his crew. Capt. Pierce was master of the situation from the moment the boat struck and that the passengers were gotten off without a single mishap is due mainly to his coolness in directing the work.

The Aftermath

The raising of the great steamer was a never-to-be-forgotten epic of Penobscot Bay sea lore.
—John Richardson, Steamboat Lore of the Penobscot

Second Mate George Williams remained with the ship overnight, along with other crewmembers. (Captain Pierce had been summoned to company headquarters in Boston.) The next day, Williams came ashore and reported that *City of Rockland* "was resting easily on the ledge and that nothing had occurred of movement during the night." Williams stated that he thought there was a good possibility that the steamer could be refloated since the principal damage was confined to "a fracture of the hull." The engine, he said, "had sustained very little damage."

An advance guard of the salvage crew arrived on Thursday, July 28, and after a preliminary examination, it was felt that the ship could be saved if the weather held. One of the divers, D.W. Brooks, made a curious discovery when he was examining the hull beneath the waves. At one point, he found himself standing on the skeleton of the steamer *City of Portland* that was wrecked on the same ledge in 1884. The *Rockland Daily Star* reported that Brooks discovered a stateroom key marked *City of Portland* and, nearby, a shaving mug "with a luxuriant growth of submarine whiskers."

Tugs, a wrecking lighter and the underwriters arrived from Boston on Friday, July 29, and by the weekend, a salvage fleet of twenty-five boats was spread around the stricken ship. Despite a heavy swell that developed in the Muscle Ridge Channel, divers were able to patch the large hole in the starboard side, pontoons were attached and seawater was pumped out of the hull before it was towed to Rockland. Richardson described *City of Rockland*'s return as "a triumphal procession with the salvage fleet, cottagers, shore whistles and the excursion steamers all making an uproar."

City of Rockland spent the next few days on the beach near the Five Kilns in Rockland Harbor undergoing temporary repairs. When the ship's builder, William McKie, arrived from Boston, he issued the following statement after examining the hull: "She is very badly damaged. In fact I have never seen a craft so shaken up."

A week after "An Encounter with Upper Gangway Ledge," *City of Rockland* was deemed fit to be moved to the William McKie yard in east Boston, where it had been built. The big steamship proceeded slowly down the coast, accompanied by two tugs. (It is not clear from newspaper reports

Three days after hitting Upper Gangway Ledge, pontoons were attached to *City of Rockland*'s hull, and the ship was towed to Rockland. *Courtesy of Penobscot Marine Museum.*

whether the ship was towed or moved under its own power.) Company officials stressed that repairs would take months and not to expect *City of Rockland* to be back in service before the following spring. It was estimated that a refit would cost $50,000.

City of Rockland did return to service the next spring, although the Eastern Steamship Company was faced with numerous claims for lost goods and luggage. Rockland agent Raphael Sherman was quoted as saying, "There are enough claims piling in to bankrupt the company."

For the next few weeks, company officials scoured the area for lost trunks and freight. In time, it was able to recover a considerable amount of the "misplaced baggage" from reluctant coastal residents with the aid of the police. One of the better stories involved a local fisherman who was passing Monroe Island when he heard the sounds of a piano thumping out over the water. He reported this to Agent Sherman, who, sure enough, was on the lookout for a missing piano.

Part III

A Tale of Two Schooners

NEPTUNE'S BRIDE: "A MELANCHOLY SHIPWRECK IN PENOBSCOT BAY"

It was the proverbial "dark and stormy night" when the ninety-ton fishing schooner *Neptune's Bride* ran on the rocks of Malcolm Ledge in southern Penobscot Bay on September 22, 1860. The outcropping lies midway between Wood Ball Island and Seal Island, thirteen miles south of Vinalhaven Island and eighteen miles off the coast of Maine. (Today the area has a reputation as a prime location for fishing and bird watching.)

Under the command of ship's master Jacob Olsen, the schooner was returning from a successful cruise in the Gulf of Maine. It was heading for its homeport of Gloucester, Massachusetts, with a hold filled with 105 barrels of mackerel. *Neptune's Bride* was a new ship described by the *Republican Journal* as "a first class vessel," valued at $5,000 and insured for $3,500. In what was obviously terrible weather (one report called it a "gale" and another a "storm"), the schooner was "jogging along under foresail" when disaster struck at about 10:00 pm.

Only two members of the thirteen-man crew would survive the wreck, and it is because of Joseph Marsh and Henry Johnson that we know what happened. Except for the watch, the crew had gone below for the night

Neptune's Bride ran on Malcolm Ledge on the night of September 22, 1860. The ledge is seen here at half tide. Wooden Ball and Matinicus islands are visible the distance. *Author's collection.*

when *Neptune's Bride* hit the rocks. As soon as the ship struck Malcolm Ledge, the men rushed on deck and made for the vessel's single dory. Fog and rain hampered the launching, but the dory was finally put over the side, and eleven crewmembers jumped in.

The heavy seas soon swamped the dory, and the eleven occupants were forced to take refuge back on the exposed ledge. With a rising tide and a heavy sea, the stranded seamen realized that they were doomed unless they could get back on *Neptune's Bride*. Two men, Joseph Marsh and George Norwood, had stayed on the ship rather than risk getting into the already overcrowded dory. They made several attempts to pass a line to their shipmates that unfortunately failed.

Neptune's Bride began to break up on the ledge as the storm intensified. As the waters rose around them, Marsh and Norwood watched the sea claim one after another of their shipmates stranded on the ledge until they had all been washed off and drowned. To escape the rising water, Marsh and Norwood made their way up into the ship's rigging. As he watched the water rise toward their perch high up on the mast, Joseph Marsh figured that the situation was hopeless and decided to swim for Seal Island a mile away. A short time later, George Norwood heard Marsh yell, "Oh my God," and he disappeared beneath the waves.

With thoughts of his wife and child back at his home in Gloucester, George Norwood determined to hang on as long as he could. The tide seemed to follow him as he climbed higher up the ship's mast. First the water rose to his feet, then his knees and then to his waist. At about 3:00 a.m., in the middle of a lightning storm, Norwood realized that he was losing consciousness and lashed himself to the mast. Then he passed out. When he came to, it was dawn; he could see that the tide was going out, and the top of the ledge was visible.

The day passed slowly for poor Norwood, who remained in his precarious perch on the mast, high above *Neptune's Bride*'s declining deck. After eighteen hours, he was suffering terribly from exposure and thirst. The prospect of spending another night on the wreck was too much for the young sailor. He later described himself as "becoming delirious," watching the tide turn and begin to creep toward him again.

Vinalhaven historian Sidney Winslow called Norwood's rescue "the merest accident." Two fishermen (we know one was named Joseph Metcalf) had been mending their nets on Seal Island. At about 5:00 p.m. on September 23, the weather cleared, and they saw the wreck of *Neptune's Bride* on Malcolm Ledge about one mile away. One of the fishermen insisted that he saw a man on the topmast. His partner told him that he was imagining things, but he was persuaded to row over and take a look. As the two men drew near, to their surprise, they saw poor Norwood clinging to the mast, more dead than alive.

They rowed the now-hallucinating Norwood across the water to their fishing shack on Seal Island, put him to bed with hot stones under his feet and gave him a strong drink of tea laced with whiskey. The next day, Norwood felt better, so Metcalf and his partner took him to Vinalhaven, where he was given medical attention and was put up in the town's hotel. He remained there until he had recovered his strength and could return home to his family. From there, Sidney Winslow wrote, "he could tell of his peril that night and of his wonderful escape."

At the time he was rescued, Norwood believed that he was the only survivor of *Neptune's Bride* disaster. As previously mentioned, there was another survivor. Henry Johnson was one of the eleven members of the crew who jumped into the dory when *Neptune's Bride* ran on the rocks. When the dory swamped, Johnson's shipmates headed for what they thought was the relative safety of Malcolm Ledge. Johnson, however, decided that the dory offered him a better chance to survive.

The dory was practically awash, but by bailing hard, Johnson managed to reduce the water level. When a few empty hogshead tubs (big barrels) from the stricken schooner floated by, Johnson grabbed them and fastened one to each side of the boat. The result was improved buoyancy for his beleaguered craft. An additional benefit was that the tubs acted as a sea anchor, which kept the dory heading into the wind. In spite of the storm, the boat took on very little water.

Johnson estimated that at about 3:00 a.m., he fell asleep in the bottom of the dory, overcome with fatigue. For the next few hours, he drifted around Penobscot Bay, oblivious to the storm or to his whereabouts. The dory continued to stay afloat, supported by the hogshead tubs that Johnson had fastened to its sides.

When the storm subsided the next morning, the exhausted Johnson was jolted awake by the following cry: "Ahoy, on the boat. Stand by to board." The lookout on a passing schooner heading for Belfast had observed an odd-looking craft in the water with a man blissfully asleep in it. It was the schooner *Anne* under the command of Captain Henderson.

Johnson could hardly believe his good fortune, for he had resigned himself to drowning in the rough waters between Matinicus Island and Vinalhaven. As the schooner *Anne* drew closer, however, he realized that he was not dreaming. Crouching in the stern of the dory, he jumped into the arms of four husky fishermen, who lifted him to safety.

When Johnson reached Belfast the next day, he was surprised and delighted to hear that George Norwood had also survived the wreck of *Neptune's Bride*. He was distressed, however, when he found out that they were the only members of the crew who had not perished in the waters around Malcolm Ledge.

ALICE E. CLARK GOES OFF COURSE

On a pleasant midsummer afternoon in 1909, Captain Britt Pendleton and his daughter, Arline, were fishing off Hewes Point on Islesboro as they watched the schooner *Alice E. Clark* sail past. After admiring the beautiful sight, Pendleton remarked, "Seems she is a mite close. Ought to be out in the bay further." When he took a closer look, Captain Britt shouted to his daughter, "She is heading right for Coombs Ledge!"

Captain Pendleton was not the only resident of Islesboro who saw the schooner heading for the rocks. The vessel was sailing up Penobscot Bay, in a moderate breeze, bound for Bangor with a full load of coal, when observers on the shore saw the ship lurch and then stop moving as its bow lifted out of the water. On board, the crew felt the vessel shudder and heard the crunch of stove-in planking of timbers and the sound of water rushing into the hold.

Coombs Ledge today is called Long Island Ledge and is covered by eight feet of water at low tide. It was noted on the chart and also marked with a buoy. In a *Down East* magazine article he wrote about the wreck, Donald Rogers noted, "Had *Alice E. Clark* been half a boat's length away in any direction, she would have cleared the ledge." In other words, there was plenty of deep water on either side.

The Builders

The Percy and Small Shipyard in Bath, Maine, built *Alice E. Clark* in 1898. The yard was established in 1894 when Captain Samuel Percy and Frank Small formed what would become a famous partnership. Over the years, the yard built seven six-masted schooners and fifteen five-masters. *Alice E. Clark* was the fourth of nineteen four-masters that the yard built.

Samuel Percy and Frank Small would go on to construct the largest wooden vessels built in North America, including the huge, 392-foot six-master *Wyoming*, which was launched in 1909. In addition, the firm built numerous smaller vessels between 1894 and 1920. Percy and Small were particularly noted for innovations in design and production that pushed the limits of wooden shipbuilding.

The firm was also involved in the repair work for ships that were damaged by collisions, fires or other catastrophic events. At the same time, Percy and Small had a fleet of sixteen vessels that traded up and down the Atlantic coast.

Under the direction of master shipbuilder Miles Merry, it took the boatyard six months to build *Alice E. Clark*, and no expense was spared to equip it with the latest conveniences. The vessel carried 6,700 feet of canvas and was fitted with a new Hyde engine windlass to raise the two anchors that weighed 5,100 pounds.

Accommodations for officers and a crew of eleven were reportedly "most comfortable." The ship had a spacious saloon (main cabin), as well as a heated cabin and a bathroom with hot and cold water for the captain and his wife, who also planned to live on board. A special feature was an electric bell with nine push buttons for communications all over the ship.

Alice E. Clark was named for the captain's wife and was launched on January 29, 1898. According to the *Bath Independent*:

> *The launching was carried out without a hitch and vessel slid onto the Kennebec River amid the cheers of a crowd of spectators and a large company of guests...*
>
> *The vessel was christened by the daughter of the owner J.S. Winslow of Portland. A number of Bath people were served a fine spread of coffee and fruit while the Clark was attended by the tug Adelia and towed to Woodward's wharf. The Clark is a craft that is worthy of a place in the front rank of wooden vessels.*

Initially, the vessel was chartered to carry coal from Norfolk, Virginia, to Bangor, Maine. For the next eleven years, the elegant four-masted schooner would sail the Atlantic coast, transporting cargos of coal in its spacious hold. The ship originally cost $64,000, although at the time of the accident, its value was probably closer to $50,000. As anticipated, the 227-foot vessel became the flagship of the fleet of ships owned by the J.S. Winslow Company of Portland.

Alice E. Clark to the Rescue

Unquestionably, *Alice E. Clark*'s finest hour came on November 1, 1898, when, eighteen miles off Cape Charles, Virginia, lookouts sighted the burning freighter *Croatan*. The steamer, which belonged to the Clyde Line, was under the command of Captain Hale. It was headed for Wilmington, North Carolina, from New York City with a general cargo, eight passengers and eighteen crew members.

A *New York Times* article, written on November 5, 1898, reported that the origins of the fire were "a mystery" to Captain Hale, but within minutes, the ship was a mass of flames. Captain Hale stated that there was no panic on board, even though *Croatan*'s lifeboats were destroyed by fire. After donning life jackets, passengers and crew quickly jumped into the sea. Unfortunately, in the process, five of the twenty-seven people on board, all members of the crew, were drowned.

When the fire was spotted, *Alice E. Clark* lay becalmed several miles away, but Captain Clark immediately sent lifeboats to rescue the survivors, who had been in the water for more than an hour. The *New York Times* reported:

> *Captain Hale, his officers, the crew and passengers gave the highest praise to Captain Clark, his wife and the crew of the Clark. They were taken on board and received every possible attention. Captain Clark not only gave the shipwrecked men and women food and clothing, but supplied them with money to take them home.*

Alice E. Clark delivered the remaining twenty-two passengers and crew of *Croatan* to Vineyard Haven, Massachusetts. The 1,024 foot *Croatan*, a member of the Clyde Line since 1891, was a total loss.

The Wreck

Eleven years later, *Alice E. Clark* was carrying 2,700 tons of bituminous coal when it ran on Coombs Ledge on July 1, 1909. Captain McDonald immediately had the sails lowered and directed the crew to save as much as they could of the ship's equipment. However, a rising tide and water pouring into the hold caused the schooner to sink rapidly, forcing the eight crewmembers to abandon the ship. All managed to escape safely. Pictures of the wreck show the bow resting on Coombs Ledge and the vessel's stern submerged.

Help was sent for, and the tug *Bismarck* arrived from Bangor but was unable to free the stricken schooner. Several days later, two lighters (barges), *Hercules* and *Leviathan*, arrived from Portland. The owners could not agree on salvage terms, however, and the lighters departed.

At the time of the accident, the *Rockland Free Press* commented, "It would seem that the only way the vessel can be saved would be by the use of pontoons, or by lashing a vessel to her on each side at low water. Then when the coal is removed she would be kept from sinking into deep water."

Three weeks later, much of the coal had been removed and dumped into the sea. Tugs had succeeded in moving the vessel slightly, but in the process, the remaining coal cargo shifted, throwing the vessel on its beam-ends and its masts into the water. John Pendleton Farrow, in his *History of Islesboro,*

Alice E. Clark is seen "hard and fast" where it ran on Coombs Ledge on the eastern side of Islesboro on July 1, 1909. *Courtesy of Penobscot Marine Museum.*

Despite salvage efforts, *Alice E. Clark* was abandoned "as lost" on December 29, 1909. *Courtesy of Penobscot Marine Museum.*

1893–1983, reported, "At that point a Boston salvage company, after an expenditure of $7,000, called it quits."

According to Farrow, after the Boston company gave up, Fields Pendleton from Islesboro bought salvage rights from the J.S. Winslow Company for $500. He first removed more coal from the *Alice E. Clark* and had it piled on the shores of Islesboro. An attempt was then made to lift the schooner off the ledge by running hawsers under the keel and positioning vessels on either side of the stricken ship to act as pontoons.

A Coast Guard cutter and two large towboats then attempted to pull the schooner off the rocks. The *Clark*'s stern swung free, but a piece of Coombs Ledge had penetrated the hull near the bow, and this kept the vessel securely pinned to the rocks. After two tries, the attempt was abandoned.

Alice E. Clark sat on Coombs Ledge for many years, while the remaining coal in its hold and in the water nearby was salvaged by Islesboro residents, as well as by passing steamboats for use in their boilers.

Part IV

Governor Bodwell

The Man and the Ship

In the spring of 1852, thirty-four-year-old Joseph Bowell left his wife and three-year-old daughter in Methuen, Massachusetts, and joined his friend Moses Webster in a quarrying venture on remote Vinalhaven Island in Penobscot Bay. Thus began the dramatic career of one of Maine's most prominent and successful nineteenth-century entrepreneurs.

The man who would become the fortieth governor of Maine was born in Methuen in 1818. As the tenth of eleven children, and the third of four sons, Joseph soon realized that he would inherit little from his father, a teamster and occasional farmer. At the age of eight, Joseph went to live with Mary, a married older sister. Mary's husband died when Bodwell was sixteen, and he briefly took a job on a nearby farm. The next year, the young man began an apprenticeship as a shoemaker.

The Industrial Revolution arrived at the town of Methuen in the 1840s, and this had a significant effect on Bodwell's life. Methuen was shortly incorporated into the newly created city of Lawrence, which was developing as a hub for the manufacture of textiles.

The plan was to build a giant dam across the Merrimac River that would generate power for textile mills. When completed, the 945-foot wall would be the longest in the world. Furthermore, its construction was expected to bring needed jobs to hundreds of stonecutters, masons and teamsters. In fact, so great was the demand for workers that laborers had to be imported from Ireland.

Vinalhaven historian Ken Reiss has analyzed the career of Joseph Bodwell, noting, "There is no record of precisely what Joseph Bodwell did

Joseph Bodwell was governor of Maine from January 5, 1887, to December 15, 1887, when he died of an apparent heart attack. *Courtesy of Vinalhaven Historical Society.*

on the building of the dam, or, for that matter, when or how long he did it." One report suggests that he may have been involved hauling stones from Pelham, New Hampshire, to Lawrence. We do know that at some point he met and became friends with a stonecutter from nearby Pelham named Moses Webster.

Webster was one year older than Bodwell and an experienced stonecutter. With a wife and growing family, Webster was anxious to establish his own granite cutting operation. Following the completion of the Lawrence dam in the early 1850s, he purchased the East Boston Quarry on Vinalhaven. Shortly afterward, he and Bodwell began a quarrying partnership that was to last more than thirty years.

Following Bodwell's death in 1887, one of the stories that circulated about the early years of the partnership was that while Moses Webster cut the stone, the future governor of Maine drove a team of oxen and shod them when necessary. Although this may have been apocryphal, it is indicative of the determination of the two young men to succeed.

It should be noted that in the nineteenth century, transporting granite from seaside quarries was more efficient than dragging heavy stones from inland quarries like Pelham, New Hampshire. This was certainly true on Vinalhaven, although the East Boston Quarry that Webster now owned had a major drawback. It was located next to a creek off Carvers Harbor that was inaccessible at low tide. This had discouraged several previous owners, but not Bodwell and Webster. The two men were not put off by the tidal limitations, and by loading their ships at high tide, they were soon transporting granite cargos for building projects up and down the East Coast.

Ken Reiss wrote, "The stone East Boston offered was remarkable. It had an exceptionally clean, straight grain that could be cut into the long, wide, thin slabs or platforms that many quarries were unable to cut, and which consequently commanded a premium price on the market."

Much of the granite from the new firm was used as paving stones in New York, Philadelphia and Washington, D.C. Precise records are hard to come by, but we know that by 1856, the Bodwell and Webster Company had become firmly established as the supplier of "platform stone" or large "flaggs" that were used for pavements in upscale urban neighborhoods before concrete came into use.

In 1871, the firm of Bodwell and Webster was reorganized as the Bodwell Granite Company, with Joseph Bodwell as the president and Moses Webster the vice-president. By this time, the company had become the dominant economic force on Vinalhaven Island, employing six hundred men in its quarry. Although it was the largest, it should be noted that the Bodwell Company was simply one of a number of granite businesses on the island.

Opposite, top: Joseph Bodwell and Moses Webster owned the East Boston Quarry. It was the largest quarry operation on Vinalhaven. Seen today, the quarry is privately owned and is filled with water. *Author's collection.*

Opposite, bottom: Moses Webster's house on Vinalhaven has served as a bed-and-breakfast for many years. *Author's collection.*

Moses Webster continued to be the on-site supervisor, while Joseph Bodwell traveled the country developing a network of contacts. Ken Reiss noted, "He opened doors to buyers in the government, especially in the Army Corps of Engineers." Almost overnight, Bodwell had blossomed into an innovative, energetic entrepreneur.

Although Webster built an impressive house on Vinalhaven, his peripatetic partner never spent more than a few days at a time on the island. Joseph Bodwell continued to live in Methuen until he moved his family in 1866 to Hallowell, where he started another granite company in partnership with William Wilson. In 1869, he was elected mayor of Hallowell.

Bodwell had an instinctive nose for a business opportunity. When a ship was only partially filled with granite, he would load the remainder of the hold with a cargo of other commodities such as hay, potatoes, corn or dried fish. When the demand for granite dried up during the Civil War, Bodwell sold hay and potatoes to the Northern army.

After the war, the Bodwell Company resumed its granite business and secured a number of lucrative government contracts, including orders for the Pennsylvania Railroad Station in Philadelphia, the U.S. Customs House in New York City, the Brooklyn Bridge and the Chicago Board of Trade, as well as slabs for the base of the Washington Monument.

Bodwell's business horizons appeared limitless. In addition to his granite enterprises, he was president of the Bodwell Water Company of Oldtown, Maine, which was the largest water power company in New England. He also carried on extensive ice and lumbering operations on the Kennebec River, he imported thoroughbred cattle from England and he was a stockholder in several railroad companies.

Joseph Bodwell traveled the country in style, but the frenetic pace of his life was beginning to wear him down physically. In early 1880s, he was talked about as a possible governor, but he declined, saying that he was too busy. In June 1886, over his protests, he was unanimously nominated as the Republican candidate for governor. That fall, he easily defeated the Democratic nominee, Clark Edwards.

Joseph Bodwell was sworn in as governor on January 5, 1887, and eleven months later, on December 15, 1887, he was dead. In spite of family cautions to slow down, he had continued to pursue his many business enterprises while also acting as governor. In fact, he engaged in several new ones, including the presidency of the New York and Boston Rapid Transit Company, whose aim was to build a railroad line between Boston and New York. As governor, Bodwell's brief administration was noted for the development of child welfare programs and the improvement of labor conditions.

Joseph Bodwell enjoyed robust health for most of his life, although his numerous business and political responsibilities were taking their toll. The governor had a warning when he experienced severe pain in his left shoulder and arm in September 1887 that apparently was a mild heart attack. Then, in early December, while he was in Brunswick waiting for a train to take him for a visit to the state prison at Thomaston, he experienced sharp chest pains. The sixty-nine-year-old chief executive lingered for a few days, but a week later, he died of what doctors described as "heart failure." It is interesting that his longtime friend and partner Moses Webster also died the same year.

Newspapers around the state eulogized the governor. The *Hallowell Register* reported, "The grief over Governor Bodwell's death is deep and sincere." The *Kennebec Journal* noted, "A man of very superior capacity, of great energy and executive ability." The *Eastern Argus* reported, "Joseph Bodwell was a man of great force of character and unquestioned integrity." The *Portland Advertiser* wrote, "Governor Bodwell was emphatically a self-made man." And the *Bangor Whig and Courier* noted, "He devoted his best energies to the promotion of the welfare of the State."

THE STEAMSHIP *GOVERNOR BODWELL*

Five years after Joseph Bodwell's death, the passenger and cargo steamship *Governor Bodwell* was built at the Gilcrist Boatyard in Rockland. It was launched in 1892 amid great fanfare. It was appropriate that a ship would be built honoring the deceased governor that would serve Vinalhaven Island for twenty-eight of the almost forty years of its existence.

The new ship was one hundred feet long with a beam of twenty-four feet. It had a freight capacity of seventy-five tons, it carried 165 passengers and was valued at $60,000, for which it was only partially insured. John Richardson wrote in *Steamboat Lore of the Penobscot*, "No Penobscot Bay steamboat has ever received the genuine affection which was universally accorded to the Governor Bodwell."

One of *Governor Bodwell*'s finest features was the speed with which it made the run from Rockland to Vinalhaven. Richardson noted, "Great was

Governor Bodwell seen leaving Carvers Harbor. It was on the Vinalhaven-Rockland route for twenty-eight of the thirty-nine years of its existence. *Courtesy of Vinalhaven Historical Society.*

the indignation of the island folk when in 1920 their beloved *Gov. Bodwell* was transferred to the longer Swan's Island run and the slower but more commodious *Vinal Haven* was placed on the short line in her stead."

A Trip on the Steamboat

The following account was written by Jane Falkins Wright in 1986 and relates a trip she took as a child in the mid-1920s on *Governor Bodwell* to Swan's Island:

> *The door opens—three people come out and turn down the street leading to the Steamboat wharf. Mother—grandmother and wee girl bouncing along between them excited by the sights-sounds-smells of a busy seaport. They make their way to the wharf where the coastal steamer, the Governor Bodwell, is waiting—destination SWANS ISLAND!!!—way off in the unknown territory of Blue Hill Bay.*

*They were soon underway leaving Rockland behind and also the
sunshine. The fog—thick and soupy—slowed this exciting voyage and
by the time they had stopped at North Haven and gone on to Stonington
they had come to a complete halt! The combination of no radar in those
days as well as fog was a real menace. Captains were cautious and so the
Governor Bodwell tied up securely for the night and all passengers made
themselves as comfortable as possible in the chairs in the salon. This
adventure made the trip all the more exciting for our wee girl—but was
of grace concern for Mother who knew not what to expect of this venture
into worlds unknown.*

*The next day the fog lifted and on they went to Swan's Island. "When
the fog lifts" became a very familiar byword ever after, as we all know. The
trip by steamer from Rockland to Swan's Island was a glorious beginning
to summer—out to sea—sailing among the beautiful islands—stopping at
North Haven and Stonington—watching freight being run by hand carts
up and down the ramp—at low tide the men hitched a rope to the dollies
and the one running down helped the one pushing up—the mewing of sea
gulls—the smell of the sea—the thrill of standing at the bow and watching
the ship cut through the waves—and often porpoises flashed in and out of
the water, following for a way—our kindly purser—Mr. Stinson—with
a special greeting each year and Capt. Kent (Rossie) welcoming us with a
nod—all became a regular part of summertime—a dreamed of Paradise
during the long winters back in Massachusetts—and each summer the
return to Swan's Island was just as wonderful as remembered.*

Not a Shaggy Dog Story

Tim Harrison in *Lighthouse Digest* magazine told the story of a big
Newfoundland dog named Nemo that was trained to answer the signals of
passing vessels by barking whenever he heard them:

*As soon as the fog began to come in he seemed to realize that he was on
duty, and went like a well-drilled soldier to his position at the extreme end
of the Heron Neck on Greens Island next to Vinalhaven. There he waited
patiently until somewhere out of the murk came the sound of a whistle or a
horn, to which he immediately responded by barking loudly.*

One captain declared that he could hear Nemo better than the foghorn on the other side of the bay. The dog never tired of his task, but remained at his station through all weather until the fog lifted, and the passing sailors could see their way again. Probably more than one vessel was saved from wreck and disaster by the timely warning of this four-footed sentinel of the sea.

Nemo seemed to distinguish some of the boats from the rest, and to bestow upon them particular attention. Thus he always saluted with special eagerness and apparent delight the steamer Governor Bodwell, on its daily trips between Vinalhaven and Rockland. It was only necessary to say in his hearing, in the most casual way, "The Bodwell is coming," and he was up and away to the shore to greet the boat; and no matter how far inland he might be, the whistle on Hurricane Island always brought him to his post on Heron Neck before it passed the light.

Naturally, Nemo was a prime favorite with those who had occasion to traverse these waters. As the local fishermen passed by in fair weather they blew their horns or whistles, and he came bounding down to the water's edge to return their salute, and to receive the biscuit and bits of meat that they threw ashore to him. That captain must have been in a great hurry, or much buffeted by head tides or contrary winds, who would not lay his course a little nearer the land for the sake of showing appreciation of the worth and services of this shaggy friend in need.

Alas, the days of the elderly steamship were drawing to a close. Prior to his death, Governor Joseph Bodwell had experienced several warnings to slow down before his fatal heart attack in December 1887. The same might be said for his namesake, the ship, when it ran on Spindle Ledge off Swan's Island in 1924 and was nearly lost. And call it a coincidence, but the length of time Joseph Bodwell and Moses Webster worked together (from the late 1840s to 1887) was the same as the lifespan (1892–1931) of the steamship *Governor Bodwell*. Both periods of time were a shade under forty years.

The beloved old boat suffered a major accident on January 27, 1924. A severe storm had delayed the delivery of the mail to Swan's Island for several days. As he approached the island, Captain Roscoe Kent reported, "It was blowing a gale from the west, the temperature was below zero, the vapor was flying thick and it was very dark." I would add that the entrance to Old Harbor on the south shore of Swan's Island had to be navigated carefully in a winter storm for a ship the size of *Governor Bodwell*.

A *Rockland Courier Gazette* account of the accident noted that the Halibut Ledge bell buoy was not functioning properly (it had turned

Governor Bodwell ran on Spindle Ledge at the entrance to Old Harbor on Swan's Island on January 27, 1924. *Courtesy of Vinalhaven Historical Society.*

upside down), so that Captain Kent had to "feel his way along." When a sudden snow squall struck, the ship lost its bearings and ran hard on Spindle Ledge, located at the entrance to Old Harbor between Harbor Island and Hockamock Head. The impact drove the bow of the ship thirty feet out of the water, and the stern began to settle.

Distress signals were sounded, and Swan's Island fishermen quickly arrived and took off the passengers along with the mail. Captain Kent and the crew remained on board for several hours and made desperate efforts to free the stricken ship. Heavy seas continued to pound the vessel, and it began to fill with water. At about midnight, the captain realized that further efforts were futile, and the crew abandoned ship.

No lives were lost, although all hands suffered from exposure and frostbite, being soaked to the skin in icy water with a temperature of twelve degrees below zero. Captain Kent reported, "The crew lived up to the noblest traditions of the sea. The wreck was the result of unforeseen and unavoidable accidents."

One month later, however, *Governor Bodwell* was miraculously back in the water. Local boatyard owner Captain John Snow had carefully brought the waterlogged hulk into the shallow waters on the Minturn side of Old Harbor, where the aging vessel was found to be less damaged than first believed. Temporary repairs were made at Snow's yard, and the ship was returned to Rockland for a full refit. By June, *Governor Bodwell* was on line, spruced up with a new cabin and ready for the summer schedule.

Disaster struck again on the evening of March 23, 1931, when *Governor Bodwell* had just arrived at Swan's Island. The vessel was tied up at the wharf for the night when a fire was discovered at 8:30 p.m. that had apparently broken out around the boiler. The fire spread rapidly so that the few crewmembers remaining on board barely got off before flames engulfed the ship.

John Richardson described the scene:

> *In a matter of minutes Old Harbor was bright as day from the devouring flames and Gov. Bodwell's doom was sealed beyond the shadow of a doubt. The gathering islanders stood helplessly by as the lines were cast off and the fiercely blazing craft was towed clear of the threatened wharf structure by a motorboat.*

The *Rockland Courier Gazette* reported, "The ship was a total loss as it burned to the water's edge and the hull then sank to the bottom." Investigations the next week found little to salvage. The hull was burned so completely that the engine had gone through the bottom of the boat. At the same time, the boiler had capsized and fallen over the side. As noted previously, *Governor Bodwell* was underinsured. Company president William White announced that it would cost $110,000 to build a modern boat equipped with a diesel engine.

Although a temporary replacement was put on the route, the *Courier Gazette* lamented, "The *Bodwell* has been a good old scout all these years, and her fate almost seems like a personal loss." John Richardson added, "One of the few items salvaged was the *Governor Bodwell*'s full-toned whistle, which was repaired and put on her successor, the steamer *North Haven*." Some folks said that the original tone was not quite right, but with the wind in the right direction, others said it stirred the memories of the gallant old ship.

Part V

The Concrete Ship

SS Polias

L arkin Post lives in Owls Head, Maine, and works for a computer company in Camden, Maine. While he was a student at East Carolina University in the late 1990s, Larkin was searching for a subject for his master's thesis. At one point, his father told him the story of the concrete ship *Polias*, which was wrecked off Port Clyde in 1920. (Post admitted at first that he thought his father meant that the ship's cargo was concrete.) The senior Post is a retired Coast Guardsman who, for several years, was stationed at Burnt Island, near the site

Polias shown underway in October 1919. The ship was built by the Fougner Concrete Shipbuilding Company. *Courtesy of Larkin Post.*

of the wreck. When he told his son the story, Larkin jumped at the idea. (Post's thesis was a valuable source for what follows.)

Views differ as to the origins of the name *Polias*. Rockland writer Kendall Merriam noted in the April 1971 issue of *Down East* magazine that the name came from the Greek goddess Athena. In her role as a protector of the city (polis), many people throughout the Greek world worshiped Athena as *Athena Polias*. There was also a 2001 article in the *Rockland Courier Gazette* by Steve Rzasa that noted that *Polias* is the Norwegian word for Polaris, the northern star.

THE WRECK

On a stormy night in February 1920, the brief career of perhaps the most unique ship ever to sail in Maine waters came to an end. The winter of 1919–20 was one of the worst on record for mid-coast Maine. On February 4 and 5, a severe blizzard struck the coast. Winds of seventy-five miles per hour ripped down power lines, halted trains and stranded passengers. Portland was blanketed with snow that reached second-story windows, and Rockland Harbor was one of many harbors so icebound that the Coast Guard had to be called to clear a channel.

In spite of the severe northeast gale, Captain Richard Coughlan of *Polias* ordered his ship to leave its dock at Searsport on Friday morning, February 6. *Polias* was in ballast (no cargo) and proceeded across Penobscot Bay heading for Norfolk, Virginia, to pick up a load of coal. *Polias* did not have a pilot on board, and Captain Coughlan, who had made the run three times in the last two months, felt that the safest route was to take the inside channel between Metinic Island and the mainland.

"We ought to be clear now," said Coughlan to the chief engineer, John Brown, shortly before he went below to get something to eat in the late afternoon. Fifteen minutes later, running at a speed of ten knots, *Polias* grounded on Old Gilley Ledge, off Port Clyde. The question was raised as to why the captain had maintained the ship's speed in the heavy seas. A possible answer was that Coughlan felt that his unusual ship handled the bad weather better at a higher speed. In any case, in the middle of the storm, Coughlan felt that it was even more dangerous to turn back. Whatever the reason, *Polias* suddenly came to a grinding stop.

Captain Richard T. Coughlan was master of *Polias* when the ship hit Old Gilley Ledge on February 6, 1920. *Courtesy of Dwyn Coughlan Raymond.*

It has also never been satisfactorily explained why *Polias* was at least an eighth of a mile off course. In the captain's defense, at the time of the grounding, visibility was severely limited by snow squalls that created whiteout conditions. Navigation and whistle buoys were so covered with ice that several had sunk in the channel or had become inoperable. There is also speculation that the compass was thrown off by a seaman with metal in his pocket standing too close to the instrument.

When *Polias* struck the ledge, it opened a gaping hole in the bottom of the hull. Coughlan immediately ordered the engines stopped and told John Harding, the radio operator, to send out distress signals. Meanwhile, the ship's momentum had carried it well onto the reef. When the ship's officers gathered on the bridge, it was decided to swing out the lifeboats but not to launch them. Coughlan then gave specific orders that, for the moment, all thirty-eight members of the crew were to stay on the ship. His thinking was that rescue by another ship was preferable to heading for the shore in lifeboats in the stormy seas.

Coughlan then tried to back *Polias* off the ledge, which made a screaming noise as the hull scraped against the rocks. As the stricken ship pitched and rolled on the reef, some of the crew panicked, convinced that it was about break to pieces. "It's sure death here," said one seaman. In defiance of the captain's orders, eleven terrified sailors, led by the third mate, Gustav Kairath, lowered a thirty-eight-foot metal lifeboat and rowed away from the ship. Although all of the men were wearing life jackets, they were never seen again.

An inspection of the damage showed flooding in the forward part of the ship, but the after part remained intact. In his thesis, Larkin Post concluded,

Polias shortly after grounding. The pounding of the waves has taken off some of the ship's paint, but the vessel still appears relatively intact. *Courtesy of Doug Lee, from his collection of John I. Snow photographs.*

"It could have been much worse." The remark heard on all sides when word that eleven lives had been lost was "what a pity the eleven men did not stick to the ship."

A Ship Born of Necessity

At the start of World War I, the United States was faced with a critical lack of cargo vessels. This shortage dated back to the Civil War, when Southern raiders had destroyed much of the Union merchant fleet. The situation also did not improve following the war, when the nation was focused primarily on developing the country's infrastructure, especially railroads. The result was that by the time World War I broke out in 1914, the United States merchant fleet ranked a mere twentieth in the world.

Although the United States did not enter the war until 1917, the nation quickly became a crucial supplier to the Allied war effort. German U-boats were sinking British shipping at an alarming rate, and this forced the United States to expand its merchant fleet to increase the quantity of goods flowing to Europe.

The introduction of the convoy system helped protect the beleaguered British merchant fleet, but without American maritime support, the Central Powers would eventually have worn the Allies down.

Thus the need for building inexpensive cargo vessels was born. In his *Down East* article on the "Wreck of the Concrete Steamer *Polias*," Kendall Merriam wrote, "When a plan was proposed to build concrete ships at half the cost, using one-third of the steel required for an ordinary steamship, it was quickly adopted." President Woodrow Wilson authorized the program after reading a report that concrete ships would be economically and structurally sound. There was even the suggestion that concrete ships could better withstand torpedo damage, although this was never proven. *Polias* was one of twelve cargo ships ordered by the United States government during World War I. Ironically, none of the twelve was launched until after the war.

In his thesis, Larkin Post wrote, "The term concrete, or cement ship, is a bit of a misnomer. A more appropriate term is a ferro-concrete vessel, since in truth such vessels were steel ships with concrete filling the holes in their steel lattice hulls." The concept of building ferro-concrete vessels did not originate in the United States. During the war, a number of European countries, as well as China, constructed concrete vessels, although the United States was the only country to adopt the concept on a grand scale.

The earliest-known concrete, or cement, watercraft was a dinghy built by Joseph Lambot in France in 1848 that was later featured in the Exposition Universelle in Paris in 1855. Beginning in the 1860s, ferro-concrete barges were built in Europe for use on canals, and in about 1896, an Italian engineer, Carlo Gabellini, began building small ships out of ferro-cement. Larger ferro-concrete barges began to be made in Germany, England, the Netherlands and Norway between 1908 and 1914.

Then a Norwegian engineer, N.K. Fougner, built an eighty-four-foot, four-hundred-ton concrete fishing vessel in 1917. This served as a prototype for four motorized concrete vessels that the Norwegian built before he and his brother moved their operation to the United States, where they felt their ideas had a better chance of being accepted on a larger scale. Fougner found a number of individuals in Washington who were receptive to his ideas. One was an engineer-physicist, Rudoph J. Wig, who undertook a feasibility study for the ferro-concrete concept.

Predictably, there was opposition to the idea from the tradition-bound nautical community, where any unusual design aroused skepticism. Many naval architects were suspicious of using such an unproven material for the design and building of ships. Then there were those who criticized (unfairly) the idea as an attempt to boost the stock of the faltering cement industry. Finally, there were those who raised questions about the type of engines that would be used to power the ships.

Some of the critics' concerns proved justified. Concrete ships proved to be heavy and uneconomical when compared to steel hulls. On average, they were 39 percent heavier and carried 5 percent less cargo than a similarly sized steel ship. As it turned out, most concrete ships had a lifespan of less than a year.

Sailors disliked concrete ships because they "felt different" compared to more traditional vessels. Barney Burnett was a crewmember on *Polias* prior to the accident. He later wrote, "I noticed how stiff the concrete ship was. She never rose to the sea, but just plowed through it rigidly. She was a war emergency vessel that I felt was dangerous." Interestingly, Burnett and a shipmate left *Polias* the day before the vessel's fatal grounding on Old Gilley Ledge.

The first concrete ship to be built in America was the privately financed *Faith*, launched in Redwood City, California. Larkin Post noted, "*Faith* proved a capable vessel and may have been the most successful of the concrete ships. It made numerous voyages, including several transatlantic trips and performed equal to her steel counterparts." Wig and other government officials followed *Faith*'s construction carefully before proceeding to build two prototype ships, *Polias* and *Atlantus*.

THE CONSTRUCTION OF *POLIAS*

Atlantus was the first of the experimental ships to be completed, and it was launched in January 1919. *Polias* was built by the Norwegian designer N.K. Fougner in his shipyard in Flushing Bay, New York, in 1918, and it was launched in May 1919. At first, Fougner simply called his design the 3,500-ton Concrete Ship.

An article in the July 1962 issue of *American Neptune* describes the construction of *Polias* as "rather simple." What follows is a paraphrasing of the "simple" process. First, outside forms were built, and then inside forms were erected. Steel reinforcing rods were inserted between the forms along with two layers of steel lattice. A special mixture of ultralight Portland cement was then poured between the layers of lattice. Following this, workers pressed pneumatic air hammers against both sides of the molds to settle the concrete into place. The effect was twofold. First, it forced the concrete around the steel reinforcements. Secondly, it forced air bubbles out of the mix, which made the cement stronger and more regular. The total pouring time for a vessel varied depending on the size of the ship, but it rarely exceeded one hundred hours.

The concrete normally cured in twenty-eight days, at which point the forms were removed. The finished hull was given two coats of spar varnish and a layer of antifouling paint before the concrete ship was launched. In the case of *Polias*, it was towed up Long Island Sound to Providence, Rhode Island, where its engine, boilers and other machinery were installed, as well as a wooden deckhouse.

Many lessons were learned during *Polias*'s construction, not the least of which was that the chilly temperatures of a New York winter slowed the curing of the ship's hull. By comparison, *Atlantus*, which was begun *after* *Polias* and was built in Wilmington, North Carolina, was completed four months *before* its sister ship. Henceforth, the government decided to locate all concrete shipyards in the southern part of the country. *Polias*'s builder, N.K Fougner, remained active in the concrete ship program until 1921, when he retired to focus exclusively on ship design.

The 267-foot-long, 2,565-ton *Polias* cost $950,000 to build. It was fitted with a triple-expansion steam engine, enabling the ship to average ten knots per hour on its sea trials. The ship was found to be seaworthy if a bit sluggish. Although it was heavier than a comparable steel ship, the *Polias*'s hull of smooth concrete had an advantage over steel hulls in that there were no rivets to cause drag, nor did it vibrate when underway. The vessel was leased to the New York and Puerto Rico Steamship Company to haul coal. *Polias* would make four voyages from December 1919 to February 1920 before its deadly encounter with Old Gilley Ledge.

THE RESCUE OF *POLIAS*

Interestingly, the naval wireless station at Otter Cliffs, on the northern end of Penobscot Bay, was the first to pick up Captain Richard Coughlan's distress call. Word was quickly relayed to the Coast Guard cutter *Acushnet* in Rockland Harbor. *Acushnet* had just returned from an exhausting two-week ice breaking patrol as far as Nova Scotia, and most of the crew was on leave recovering from the ordeal. The lifeboat station at Burnt Island had also seen the lights of *Polias* but had not taken action because it failed to see the distress rockets fired from the ship. The thought was that *Polias* had simply anchored to ride out the storm.

In Rockland, *Acushnet's* Captain Lauriat sounded the ship's whistle and asked the police to help round up his crewmen. (Some were in bars, and others were at the local skating rink, where they had gone for some well-deserved recreation.) The rest, however, were in the hospital. When those who were healthy returned to *Acushnet*, the lack of manpower was deemed critical. Twenty-one sailors were simply too ill to join the ship, following their exposure to the severe weather the ship had encountered. Captain Lauriat himself was being treated for symptoms of the flu.

The cutter *Acushnet* left Rockland Harbor in the late morning so short of men that Lauriat decided to stop at the Whitehead Lifesaving Station on the Mussel Ridge Channel for reinforcements. After considerable delays, Lauriat was able to add six men to his crew at Whitehead before proceeding to the site of the wreck at Old Gilley Ledge. Weather conditions were so bad that *Acushnet* was unable to locate *Polias* and sailed four miles past the distressed ship.

Acushnet backtracked until the cutter's crew finally spotted flares from *Polias*. Captain Lauriat did not want to get too close to the wreck and therefore anchored his vessel half a mile away in twenty fathoms of water. Meanwhile, a six-man crew from the nearby Burnt Island Lifesaving Station had broken through the ice surrounding the island and joined the rescue effort. Rescue operations finally got underway, and four lifeboats headed for *Polias*. Two hours later, amid heavy seas and freezing temperatures, the remaining twenty-seven *Polias* crewmen were safely hoisted aboard *Acushnet*, where they received food and warm clothing.

Before returning to Rockland, Captain Couglan insisted on looking for the eleven crewmen who had left the ship against his orders. The ensuing search lasted nine hours and turned out to be futile. *Acushnet* commenced a zigzag course toward Monhegan Island, seven miles away, which was the direction the errant crewmen were seen heading. Upon reaching Monhegan, *Acushnet* turned toward Rockland, all the while continuing a zigzag search pattern. It was finally agreed that the fierce northeasterly winds had blown the lifeboat out to sea and its occupants had died of exposure. The only remains that were ever found of the lost lifeboat were three life jackets, an oar and a boat hook that were discovered on Monhegan later in the year.

In Rockland, eight members of the *Polias* crew were hospitalized, while the remainder found accommodations in boardinghouses until they were paid off and could return home. Captain Coughlan established himself in the Thorndike Hotel, where he was faced with the grim task of writing a wreck report. There were many questions to be answered from the disaster in which a valuable ship was wrecked and eleven crewmen lost.

Richard Coughlan was later tried at the Customs Court in Portland, where he pled guilty to not having a pilot on board. He was fined $100 for the violation. It should be noted that in 1920, this was a substantial fine, possibly as much as half of the captain's monthly salary.

Otherwise, Coughlan was exonerated. The subsequent investigation by a board of inquiry determined that the wrecking of *Polias* was an accident. Coughlan would maintain throughout his life that he had done all he could to prevent loss of life and that the eleven men had left the ship under his protests. Later, the New York and Puerto Rico Steamship Company dismissed a lawsuit by the wife of the lost third mate, Gustav Kairath, as having no validity.

At Home on Old Gilley Ledge

Polias spent many years sitting on Old Gilley Ledge. The weight of the ship and the fact that it was driven onto the ledge at full speed had made the vessel virtually part of the rock. As John Richardson wrote in *Steamboat Lore of the Penobscot*, "Nature finally did the wrecking job."

The United States Shipping Board (USSB) sent a team to look into the possibility of salvage. Divers found a number of large holes in the ship's hull, and after a two-day survey, the T.A. Scott Wrecking Company from New London, Connecticut, declared the ship a total loss. Although the hull was damaged beyond repair, valuable equipment remained above board, and this kept interest in the wreck alive.

Charles Ludlow, a New York attorney, was one who was interested. He planned to refloat the ship by sealing the hatches and pumping compressed air into the hull. Ludlow hoped that this would provide enough lift to drag the vessel off the ledge. He then proposed to tow it to a dry dock, where it would be stripped of its fixtures. After four months of work by a sixteen-man crew and at a cost of $24,000, Ludlow's team

Polias aground on Old Gilley Ledge, circa February 15, 1920. The photograph was taken at extremely high tide. *Courtesy of Hap Willson.*

Polias's foredeck being inspected following the wreck. Note the snow on the bridge and on the cargo booms. *Courtesy of Doug Lee, from his collection of John I. Snow photographs.*

was unsuccessful. Unwilling to admit defeat, the determined lawyer was granted an extension. After two years of repeated failures, the frustrated Ludlow was finally forced to give up.

Over the years, *Polias* became an object of interest to thousands of spectators who viewed the wreck as it sat on Old Gilley Ledge. Eventually, a winter storm washed the hull off the ledge into deeper water. Once *Polias* slid under the waves, it more or less went to pieces. Larkin Post said that local divers have recovered a propeller and the ship's anchors. Port Clyde natives have also salvaged bits and pieces, including the ship's china and the ship's whistle, which is on display at the Marshall Point Lighthouse Museum.

SS *Polias* is still marked on navigation charts today. And at extremely low tide, a portion of the bulkhead can be seen sitting on the Old Gilley Ledge two miles off Port Clyde.

Part VI

The Portland Gale Hits Penobscot Bay

The weather report for November 26, 1898, showed two high-energy, low-pressure masses converging on New England. One was a cold front moving eastward from Canada and the Great Lakes. The other, a front filled with humidity, was heading up the coast from the south. What the weathermen of the day could not have predicted was that the collision of these two systems would result in one of the great disasters in maritime history, the infamous nor'easter known as the Portland Gale.

On land, the storm caused almost the entire suspension of railway traffic throughout New England. In Maine, eight inches of snow fell in Waterville, and trains were stalled. A relief train was sent to Brunswick, and the crew reported snowdrifts ten to fifteen feet along the line. In Lewiston and Augusta, snow made the streets impassable, and in Bangor, railway service was paralyzed. The crew on a train from Waterville for Belfast got a nasty surprise. As the train was crossing the Unity Pond Bridge with a snowplow mounted on the front, the plow derailed and slid out onto the ice, damaging the bridge. The train barely got across safely.

At sea, the Portland Gale caused 450 deaths, wrecked four hundred ships and was one of the most treacherous storms to ever hit the New England coast. One hundred years later, the papers were still writing about the "Portland Storm," as it was also called. At the time, the *Boston Globe* described it as "the measuring stick with which all subsequent storms would be measured." John Richardson would later write in *Steamboat Lore of the Penobscot*, "No storm made such an impression."

This is not to suggest that the Portland Gale should stand alone. Hundreds of lives have been lost in storms on the Maine coast since *Angel Gabriel* ran on the rocks at Pemaquid in an August hurricane in 1635. Joseph Williamson's *History of Belfast* calls the Portland Gale "a pretty tough storm but it was not the worst ever experienced here." According to Edward Snow, the November Gale of 1950 was also devastating. In his book *Great Gales and Dire Disasters*, Snow wrote:

> *When the storm* [November Gale] *struck the Maine coast and islands were subject to a worse buffeting than ever before in the twentieth century. Out at the lighthouses the havoc was terrible. At Matinicus Rock, Saddleback Ledge and Mt Desert Rock Portland giant waves swept away walks, ramps, huts, hencoops and everything else that was not secured inside the main buildings.*

The Portland Gale takes its name from the sinking of the luxury side-wheeler *Portland*, which left Boston on November 26 on its overnight run to Portland. South of Gloucester, off Cape Ann, the ship sank in ninety-mile-per-hour winds and huge waves. Not one of the nearly 190 passengers and crew (the passenger list went down with the ship) survived the dense snow and freezing temperatures, although 36 bodies were eventually recovered.

None of the 192 passengers and crew survived the sinking of the luxury side-wheeler *Portland*. It is seen here leaving Boston Harbor. *Courtesy of Chandler Blackington.*

W. H. ROCHE.   HON. E. D. FREEMAN   JOSIAH FRYE.   RUTH FRYE,   MRS. H. M. PRAT

JOHN T. WALTON,   T. B. MERRILL,   ANSEL L. DYER,   LEWIS M. NELSON,   G. P. BON
Assistant Engineer.   Chief Engineer.   Quartermaster.   Second Pilot.

THESE WERE PASSE
Portraits of some of the persons

This newspaper article is a memorial to the passengers from the steamer *Portland* who drowned when the ship sank en route to Portland from Boston. *From the collections of Maine Historical Society/ Maine Memory Network, Item 13808.*

Questions were raised as to why a vessel that was basically a riverboat, propelled by a paddle wheel with a shallow, ten-foot draft, would venture out in such a storm. *Portland*'s construction enabled it to navigate Maine's rivers, but the steamer's high, narrow superstructure made it unstable in rough seas. Although the sky was darkening when *Portland* left Boston, the winds had not yet increased. Once the ship was underway, Captain Hollis Blanchard was faced with a dilemma. Turning the vulnerable craft around in heavy weather was out of the question, as the boat could have capsized. All he could do was to try to outrun the storm, which turned out to be futile.

Cashier at Owen's mumered

E. L. COBB.   MRS. M. A. BERRY,   MISS M. L. SYKES.   JOHN A. DILLON.   MISS S. B. HOLME.
Stewardess.

BEN HEUSTON.   JOHN H. MURPHY.   W. S. PROCTOR.   J. H. GATELY,   ORA L. LEIGHTON,
Second Steward.   Fireman.

N THE PORTLAND.
lost on the Portland, Nov. 27.

The drowning of 190 people, the majority of whom were Portlanders returning home after the Thanksgiving holidays, raised calls for a congressional investigation. One result was the gradual adoption of steel-hulled, propeller-driven ships replacing side-wheelers on ocean routes. The design of coastal steamers also began to change. Bows were raised, and the after decks were enclosed. And ship's captains began to send passenger lists ashore before departing on their runs.

Although the elegant *Portland* was the best-known vessel to sink, farther up the coast, Penobscot Bay was also hit hard. Most ships were simply overwhelmed by the force of the storm and sank. Others were destroyed when they collided with one another. Many were thrown on the rocks when their anchor lines parted. A few vessels that were initially reported lost turned up, having found a protected harbor or been towed to safety by an obliging tugboat.

There were a few passenger liners like *Portland* that went down, although the majority of vessels that sank were coastal schooners carrying cargos of coal, limestone, granite or lumber that were frequently uninsured. As will be seen, most of the ships wrecked on the rocks were condemned, although some of the cargos were saved. The effects of the Portland Gale on Penobscot Bay and its shipping is the focus of this part.

Rockland Ships

In terms of human lives, the loss of the steamer *Pentagoet* was the most costly marine disaster in the history of Rockland. The entire crew of sixteen perished when the ship sank off Cape Ann in the vicinity of the steamer *Portland*. The elderly vessel was described by a writer as "one of Saturday's children," meaning it was a hardworking ship.

Pentagoet was built in 1863 and was originally a Civil War gunboat named *Hero*. Over the next thirty-five years, the ship's name was frequently changed, as it was used for different purposes: from *Hero* (Federal gunboat) to USS *Moccasin* (U.S. Coast Guard) to *George M. Bibb* (a revenue cutter on the Great Lakes) to *Pentagoet* when it was used as a cargo steamer.

Pentagoet was a propeller-driven, wooden-hulled steamer powered by a 250-horsepower engine. It was 128 feet long with a 23-foot beam. The ship drew 16 feet and was built at a cost of $10,000. When it was purchased by the Manhattan Steamship Company in 1898, an additional $10,000 was spent to upgrade the aging steamer.

For a time, *Pentagoet* served the route between Rockland and Swan's Island, with occasional stops at Vinalhaven. Then the company directors decided to shift the vessel from the thirty-mile Swan's Island run to the long, deep-water trip from Rockland to New York City. The new owners initially found it difficult to recruit a crew, as many seamen questioned whether *Pentagoet* was up to the task. (Sailors also preferred to serve on one of the company's fleet of six newer ships.) Eventually, however, a crew was signed. Five of the sixteen men were from Maine, including the ship's captain from

The entire crew of *Pentagoet* perished when the ship sank at the height of the Portland Gale in November 1898. *Author's collection.*

Rockland. Just before the final trip, Cal Stinson from Swan's Island quit, saying prophetically, "The stick ain't worth the candle."

John Richardson wrote in *Steamboat Lore of the Penobscot*, "In spite of her detractors, *Pentagoet* was considered a good sea boat and made her long runs with clock-like regularity throughout her final year, weathering many storms when the Boston-Bangor liners remained in harbor." The ship was not licensed to carry passengers, and on its last run, its hold was filled with 160 tons of cargo to fill Rockland's stores with gifts for the coming Christmas season.

Pentagoet had the advantage of having an extremely capable captain in the person of Orris Ingraham; his twin brother, Otis, was half an hour older and equally distinguished. Both men were members of the celebrated Rockland family of sea captains. Orris was sixty-seven years old and had spent almost fifty years as a pilot and master, handling such well-known ships as *City of Richmond* and *Vinal Haven*. Orris Ingraham had a wife and two children, one of whom had died when hit by lightning while serving aboard one of his father's ships.

The steamer *Pentagoet* left New York Harbor on its last voyage on Friday, November 25, with orders to hug the coast. The ship was last spotted passing Highland Light in Massachusetts Bay at 11:00 a.m. on Sunday, November 27, in the company of another steamer, most probably the ill-fated *Portland*. "After this," Richardson wrote, "her fate is shrouded in mystery."

According to the ship's owners, one possibility is that the old steamer was "pooped" (struck from the stern) by a huge wave that swept everything away, including deckhouse, boats and hatch covers. The next few waves would have poured into the hull, sending *Pentagoet* plunging to the bottom.

Bits of *Pentagoet's* distinctive deep-red cabin were also found among the wreckage of *Portland*, fueling speculation that the two vessels may have collided. Peter Dow Bachelder and Mason Philip Smith, however, questioned this theory in their book *Four Short Blasts*. "None of the bodies from Pentagoet's crew were ever found and it seems likely had the two vessels struck, bodies from both would have come ashore, instead of just from *Portland*."

Belfast's *Republican American* and the *Rockland Courier-Gazette* reported on other Rockland-area ships that were casualties of the storm. Like *Pentagoet*, the granite-laden Rockland schooner *Addie E. Snow* was also in the vicinity of the steamer *Portland* in Massachusetts Bay when it went down with its entire crew. One possibility is that the two vessels collided as *Portland* was attempting to rescue the beleaguered schooner that was being blown out to sea. Years later, when divers discovered *Portland* in four hundred feet of water, *Addie E. Snow* was found resting on the bottom a quarter of a mile away.

The two-masted schooner *Jordan L. Mott* was under the command of Charles Dyer from Owls Head. The ship was filled with a cargo of coal when it pulled into Provincetown Harbor to avoid the gale. To prevent his father, who was part of the crew, from being washed overboard, Captain Dyer lashed him to the mast. By the time help arrived eighteen hours later, the elderly Dyer had frozen to death. The rest of the crew survived, but the vessel was a total loss.

The schooner *Island City* was heading for Massachusetts from Nova Scotia with a cargo of coal when it was hit by the storm. Captain Nelson and the entire crew of the Rockland schooner perished when the vessel went down off Martha's Vineyard. The ship was last seen off the northeastern tip of the island at the mercy of the waves, with Captain Nelson and several crewmembers desperately hanging on to the rigging. Residents of Martha's Vineyard sighted the vessel, but they were unable to provide help, as the nearest lifesaving station on the island was at Gay Head, twenty miles away.

In Rockland, the schooner *Bertha E. Glover*, its hold filled with lime, had just left the dock when it was driven ashore on the east side of Rockland Harbor. The ship sprang a leak, causing the cargo to catch fire. The fire burned the schooner to the water's edge in spite of the efforts of its crew to put it out.

The Rockland schooner *Fairy Queen* was carrying a cargo of lumber heading for Swan's Island from Bangor. When the storm split the vessel in two, its cargo was strewn along the shore. The nine-ton craft was a total loss.

The schooner *Thomas Boose* was loaded with plaster, having departed from Hillsboro, New Brunswick, heading for Newark, New Jersey. It was caught in the storm while crossing Penobscot Bay and was driven ashore at Hopper's Island near Port Clyde. The schooner was under the command of Captain Day, from Richmond, Virginia. The crew was saved, but the ship was a total loss.

One bright note was the story of the lobster smack *Fannie May*. On Sunday morning, at the height of the storm, the boat, owned by F.W. Collins, broke from its moorings and was dashed against Tillson's Wharf in Rockland, where it sank. When the vessel was refloated several days later, it was found to be in much better condition than expected.

Deer Isle's *Bessie H. Gross*

"The most tragic loss to Deer Isle in the Portland Gale was that of the schooner *Bessie Gross* which took with her two generations of the Thurston family of South Deer Isle." So wrote Deer Isle historian Clayton Gross in his book *Island Chronicles*.

Bessie H. Gross was built at Tynmouth, New Brunswick, in 1878 and was owned by Frank Warren of South Deer Isle. At the time of the November storm, the ship was on its last run of the season. Clayton Gross related that it was not unusual for the crew of a coasting vessel to use the final trip of the season to return home with a large quantity of provisions for the winter. By combining their purchasing power, seamen would be able to fill their ship's hold with staples at wholesale prices when in Boston.

The schooner *Bessie H. Gross* had left Deer Isle bound for Boston with its eight-foot-deep hold filled with 260 tons of granite. Carrying such a heavy load was a risky business for the eighty-foot vessel. The enormous weight of the stones made any shift in their position a threat to the stability of the modest-sized ship. If the granite broke loose, its pounding could open *Bessie H. Gross*'s seams.

At the helm of the doomed vessel was Captain Wallace Thurston, accompanied by his seventy-year-old father, Thomas, as well as two crewmen, Neil McDonald and Hezikiah Robbins. The elderly Thurston had gone along specifically to help with the purchase of such staples as flour, sugar, molasses and canned goods to carry Deer Isle families through the winter months.

The gale hit *Bessie H. Gross* on Saturday night, November 26, when it was off Cape Ann, and the ship was driven south for several hours. It finally struck Fresh Island Ledge, a few miles off Manchester-by-the-Sea, where it broke up, throwing the elderly Thurston into the water. When Captain John Thurston tried to get a rope around his father, he drowned as well.

The other two members of the crew, Neil McDonald and Hezekiah Robbins, managed to reach shore on nearby House Island. Unfortunately, the barren place had no food or shelter, and the marooned men remained there until help arrived on Monday morning, whereupon they were taken to the town of Manchester. Clayton Gross wrote, "Both men were in a state of collapse from cold and hunger and McDonald was in critical condition, both of his feet having been frozen." Sadly, the schooner *Bessie H. Gross* was a total loss.

ISLESBORO LOSSES

The sixty-six-ton schooner *Alida* from Bangor had the misfortune to be at anchor in Gilkey's Harbor on Islesboro when the gale hit the island. Captain Roberts put out extra lines hoping to secure his ship. The anchors held for a while, but early Sunday afternoon, the cables gave way, and *Alida* was blown out into the bay. The schooner went ashore at Lobster Cove near White Head and was a total loss.

Far to the south of Islesboro, off Provincetown, the Portland Gale took the lives of six men and destroyed three vessels from the Penobscot Bay island. The *Belfast Republican Journal* described the loss of the schooner *Lester A. Lewis* as "[t]he saddest wreck, so far as is known." The 240-ton schooner was built in Bangor in 1877 and was carrying a cargo of phosphate and guano to Bangor when it was hit by the full fury of the Portland Gale in Provincetown Harbor.

The ship appeared to be safely anchored, with its sails furled and anchors set. Under normal weather conditions, "or even in an ordinary gale, it would have been considered safe," the paper noted. However, nothing could withstand the ferocity of the storm, and the schooner broke away from its anchors, capsized and sank, along with thirty other vessels in Provincetown Harbor that were blown ashore or sunk.

With very little time to prepare for the storm, it appears that the captain and crew lashed themselves to the ship's rigging. The *Republican Journal* speculated that the three crewmembers were closer to the deck so that they must have drowned soon after the vessel sank. Captain Kimball was found lashed to the spanker boom higher up in the rigging and apparently had frozen to death.

Captain Nelson Kimball, commander of the schooner, was a forty-six-year-old native of Islesboro and had been a sailor all his life. Kimball had captained a number of sailing vessels, including the schooners *Paul Seavey* and *Nellie S. Pickering*, as well as several large coasters. A wife and two children survived him.

It is interesting that two other members of the three-man crew were also experienced mariners, as well as former ship's captains. The mate of the schooner was fifty-five-year-old Isaac Herrick, who had previously been master of two schooners and several coasting vessels. He was a native of Islesboro and left behind a wife and a daughter.

Captain Henry P. Hatch was steward of *Lester A. Lewis* and had also skippered several large coasting vessels. Each of the three "captains" were described in news reports as respected members of their island community and belonged to the Islesboro Lodge of Masons.

Islesboro sent N.L. Gilkey, son of another island seafaring family, to Provincetown with the unenviable task of identifying the remains of the sailors who had drowned in the gale. Gilkey had no difficulty in finding the bodies of the Islesboro men and described the scenes he saw in Provincetown following the storm as "heart-rending." Mr. Gilkey reported that he received "all assistance possible" from those he met, especially the Pendleton brothers from Islesboro, who had lost several vessels in the storm.

Another Islesboro ship that took a beating was the three-masted schooner *Henry R. Tilton*, under the command of Captain Cobb. The vessel was bound for Boston from Norfolk with a cargo of pine. In anticipation of the coming storm, the captain appears to have taken every precaution, including putting out two heavy chain anchors.

According to news reports, "The best of ground tackle could not withstand the terrible strain, and both chains parted and the ship went ashore near the life-saving station (now a Coast Guard station) at Point Allerton," which is outside Boston Harbor. Fortunately, the whole seven-man crew was saved. (Certainly the ship's proximity to the lifesaving station helped.) A reporter wrote, "The schooner is up high and dry and if she ever goes overboard again she will have to be launched on ways."

In addition to the four men from the *Lester A. Lewis* who died, Augustine Parker was one of the two other Islesboro sailors who perished in the gale.

During the gale, the schooner *Henry B. Tilton* was washed ashore on Stony Beach at Hull south of Boston. *Courtesy of Penobscot Marine Museum.*

Parker drowned along with two men from Lincolnville when the big iron coal barge *Delaware* lost its tow and went aground. The twenty-five-year-old seaman left a wife and child.

The other casualty was Lewis Beach, a young seaman on the schooner *Lunet*, which was coming from Perth Amboy, New Jersey, and heading for Bangor. The schooner went down with all five crewmembers, including Beach, near Tarpaulin Cove Light, south of Cape Cod.

EFFECTS ON BELFAST

When the Portland Gale hit the town of Belfast, the newspaper *Belfast Age* gave the following description of the effects of the storm:

> *The heavy storm began with strong breezes Saturday afternoon. That night it continued to increase in violence until Sunday morning. When dawn broke a wild easterly storm was raging. Limbs were broken from trees and wires were torn down making it almost impossible to have communications with the outside world.*

The greatest damage was on the waterfront with several vessels going ashore. The schooner Gazelle was at first thought to be lost but later was found having ridden out the gale in Islesboro.

Although several Belfast ships were badly battered in the Massachusetts Bay area, the storm's effects were not as severe in the town's harbor. The Belfast schooner *Charles E. Raymond*, from Bangor bound for New York, was carrying a cargo of lumber. The schooner was forced to slip its chains to prevent a collision with other craft in the harbor and went ashore just north of Norris wharf. The schooner lost its jib boom and headgear but was otherwise undamaged.

The schooner *Flora Condon* was reported dismasted and "otherwise damaged at Vineyard Haven (Martha's Vineyard) during the gale." Captain Sellers wrote to his family that he could have ridden out the gale had his ship not been run into by two schooners, both of which sank.

The collision with the second schooner carried away *Condon*'s bowsprit, following which the main mast went overboard. Fortunately, the crew escaped injury, and the hull of the *Condon* was not badly damaged. Above deck, the spars, sails, rigging and ironwork all sustained some damage. *Condon* was eventually towed to a New York shipyard, where the vessel was laid up for repairs until the following spring.

A personal loss to Belfast was the death of the previously mentioned Captain Hollis Blanchard, who drowned commanding the steamer *Portland*. Blanchard was born in Searsport, but he had been a longtime resident of Belfast. As a child young, Hollis went to sea for the first time with his father at the age of nine. He rose rapidly through the ranks to become a captain while still a young man.

Blanchard had a long and distinguished career as a ship's captain. His first job was as master of the schooner *Mary A. Coombs* from Islesboro. Further commands included the brig *R.S. Hassell* and the steamers *Cambridge* and *William Tibbetts*. Blanchard then moved on to skipper a number of coasters and other vessels in the West India trade for various Portland merchants. For the ten years prior to his death, Blanchard was employed by the Portland Steamship Company as captain of the majestic passenger liner *Portland*.

Captain Blanchard was described in his obituary as "an honorable man, a good navigator and master of his calling." His supporters claimed that it was known that *Portland* never left port without orders from the company and that Blanchard was not one to go against the orders of his superiors, especially in such bad weather. Those who knew Captain Blanchard felt that he had been unjustly blamed for the loss of *Portland*.

ELSEWHERE IN THE BAY

At FORT POINT, at the entrance to the Penobscot River, the wharf was completely destroyed by the storm. The crews of several wrecked vessels were saved, although they had a terrible time getting ashore, and some narrowly escaped drowning. Most of the men were quartered at the Fort Point light station as guests of Captain Webster, the lighthouse keeper.

The three-masted schooner *William Marshall* had an unusual experience. It was heading up the Penobscot River to Bangor to take on a cargo of ice for New York when it struck Fort Point Ledge on Friday night. There it remained until Saturday afternoon, when it was hauled off. The ship then anchored in nearby Belfast Harbor, where it survived the worst of the blow. When the schooner was pulled out a few days later, inspectors found the hull to be relatively undamaged.

At NORTHPORT, the most serious disaster was the wreck of Captain A.L. Cotton's three-masted schooner *A.B. Perry*, which had come down the Penobscot River from Bangor, heading for New York. The manifest showed that the schooner was carrying a cargo of "deals," which were wooden planks of pine, as well as fur. The 220-ton vessel had prepared for the storm by anchoring off the North Shore of Northport, two miles out of the harbor in six fathoms of water, with both regular anchors and a large kedge anchor out.

At about five o'clock Sunday morning, the schooner "dragged ashore" on Ellwell's Point. The stern hit first, and then the ship was thrown broadside onto the rocks, which badly damaged *Perry*'s keel, as well as its sternpost and rudder. Above decks, with the exception of the forward cabin, however, the ship was relatively intact. The cargo was safe except for a few pieces of lumber on deck that had washed overboard. In the midst of the turmoil, the crew got ashore safely.

When Port Warden N.S. Lord surveyed the wreck on Monday afternoon, he declared the "voyage [to] be abandoned." This gave the underwriters the cargo and the owners the vessel, which was not insured. When Captain Joel Hopkins, the underwriters' agent, arrived, he proceeded to make arrangements for reshipping the cargo of lumber.

The next day, it was found that during the course of the storm, the schooner had slid a few feet down the rocks, which facilitated pulling it all the way off. *A.B. Perry* was then towed into Belfast, where the cargo was unloaded. The owners decided not to repair the vessel, and it was sold in in its present condition.

When the storm hit CAMDEN on Saturday night, it did a great deal of damage to ships in the harbor and the waterfront. The schooner *Sandy Point*, commanded by Captain Harvey, went ashore on what is known locally as Pine Tree Ledge, below the lime kiln, and was a total wreck. A Bucksport family owned the old ship.

Captain Lane's schooner *Leona* was unloading corn for the Camden gristmill when it broke from its mooring at Johnson Knight's stone wharf and crashed against the shore, badly damaging the vessel's side. The schooner *Charles McDonald* was also badly damaged while tied up at Ogier's wharf.

On VINALHAVEN, in the middle of Penobscot Bay, the schooner *Amy Knight* from Bucksport was caught in the storm. It was bound for Boston from Bangor with a load of lumber. The ship, commanded by Captain Grant, was initially reported as missing. It was finally located in "bad condition" on December 1, having washed ashore on one of the White Islands, near Vinalhaven. The crew was reported as safe, and the men were able to save a portion of the cargo. The vessel was owned by Delano Brothers of Bucksport, although it was not insured.

THE STORM AT MOUNT DESERT

One might think that by the time the storm had crossed Penobscot Bay and headed down east, it would have begun to diminish. If so, this was not evident to the residents of Southwest Harbor. The first page of the December 1 issue of the *Belfast Republican Journal* reported the following conditions:

> *The northeast gale of Saturday night and Sunday, November 26 and 27, accompanied with snow, did considerable damage, although the sea did not run very high. Had the wind been from the east to southeast there would not have been a vessel afloat, as our harbor is exposed to those winds. The older inhabitants pronounce it the heaviest gale for twenty years.*
>
> *The snowstorm of Sunday, November 27th, was unusually severe for so early in the season, and had there been as much snow on the ground as there was on February 1st, the storm would have been fully bad. The snow began falling about 1 o'clock Sunday morning and a northeast gale blew steadily from that time until after daylight Monday morning. The wind decreased gradually but did not die out wholly until afternoon. The*

snowfall continued until well into the forenoon. The snow was drifted badly, there being long stretches of bare ground and near by drifts in some places five feet high. Traveling was bad, but the mail stages and milkmen got through all right.

On land, a large icehouse owned by J.L. Stanley and under construction at the water's edge was boarded up in anticipation of the storm. By 6:00 a.m. Sunday morning, it had blown down. In the process of falling, it struck the roof of William Ward's store as well his house. The paper reported that "it pressed it over somewhat, so that doors could not be opened, but otherwise no material damage was done."

Otherwise, relatively little damage on land was reported, although a number of vessels met with disaster in the harbor. Some examples follow:

The sixty-seven-ton schooner Venilia was built at Castine in 1867. The elderly vessel had come from Portland and was bound for Eastport, Maine, loaded with corn and oats. Venilia washed ashore at Southwest Harbor at 11:00 AM Sunday and filled with water. The crew was saved, although initial reports were that the schooner was a total wreck.

The tug *Ralph Ross* from Bangor arrived late Saturday evening towing the steamer *Sebenoa* of the Maine Central Ferry that had recently run into Crabtree Lighthouse. The two vessels tied up at the Southwest Harbor steamboat wharf during the gale. At about 3:00 p.m. Sunday afternoon, the sloop yacht *Alpha* broke from its mooring and came ashore at low water. "She is badly used up," the paper reported.

The *Republican Journal* concluded its report on the storm by noting, "There were no church bells Sunday morning or evening, which is something very unusual. There were a few people at the Baptist church in the morning and Rev. A.H. Gordon, of Ipswich, MA, gave a talk on the subject he had chosen for his sermon for that day."

Reflecting on the effects of the Portland Gale, Maine maritime historian Lawrence Allin wrote, "The loss of a ship which a man might have helped build was the loss of a small part of himself. The loss of friends he had known since childhood was the loss of a greater part of himself, for, on the Bay friends are measured as a part of one's self."

Some Other Penobscot Bay Shipwrecks

It is impossible to produce an accurate figure for the number of shipwrecks that have occurred in Penobscot Bay. Jon Johansen, editor of *Maine Coastal News*, gave us some help, however, when he cited 250 *significant* sinkings that have occurred in the Penobscot Bay area dating from colonial times to 1960. Several of the more interesting ones follow.

ROYAL TAR, OCTOBER 25, 1836

Royal Tar was a steamboat that ran between the Canadian province of New Brunswick and Portland, Maine, and sank off Vinalhaven in 1836. The 160-foot-long vessel was carrying ninety-three passengers and crew, as well as a traveling circus of two-dozen animals, when it caught fire, most likely from an overheated boiler. To accommodate the circus, *Royal Tar* was modified in ways modern safety regulations would not permit: two of the four lifeboats had been removed to make room for the animals, and there was no limit placed on the number of passengers the vessel could carry. Finally, life jackets, in the formal sense, did not exist in 1836.

When Captain Thomas Reed realized that his ship was on fire, he immediately launched the two remaining lifeboats. The animals either perished in their cages or were pushed over the side. A few passengers

Royal Tar was carrying ninety-three people and two dozen circus animals when it caught fire and sank off Vinalhaven on October 25, 1836. *Courtesy of Vinalhaven Historical Society.*

jumped into the freezing waters and either held on to the ship or attempted to swim to Vinalhaven one mile away. When a rescue ship finally appeared, other passengers were transferred to safety. In all, twenty-nine passengers and three members of the crew perished in the catastrophe. The remains of *Royal Tar* were never found.

EMPEROR, MAY 28, 1872

On a foggy spring night, the six-hundred-ton side-wheeler *Emperor* was steaming across Penobscot Bay, with Captain W.E. Sulis at the helm. The ship was bound for Portland from Nova Scotia when, a *New York Times* article reported, "it struck heavily" on Eastern Point Ledge, near Seal Island. As the wooden vessel filled rapidly with water, the eighty passengers were quickly loaded into lifeboats. When dawn broke, they spotted Matinicus Rock Lighthouse several miles away. There, the *Times* article noted, the lighthouse keeper, "Captain J.H. Gant, showed every attention in his power to the unfortunate passengers and crew." Grant sent a boat to the mainland requesting help, and a few hours later, a relief schooner arrived.

The passengers and crew were ferried to Rockland. Nothing was saved from the badly damaged *Emperor*, which was considered to be a total loss. The steamer's upper deck was torn off, and it capsized and sank on Eastern Point Ledge. Remarkably, a few months later, *Emperor* was raised from the ledge and taken to the mainland for salvage.

ULYSSES, JANUARY 11, 1878

The *New York Times* described the storm that destroyed *Ulysses* in Rockland Harbor as follows: "The heaviest northeast gale ever known here prevailed last night, doing a great amount of damage. Many buildings in this place were also unroofed." The effects on Rockland shipping, especially on *Ulysses*, were devastating. The steamer was owned by the Sullivan Line, which ran from Rockland to Mount Desert. At the height of the storm, *Ulysses* broke from its moorings and was thrown on the rocks near the South Maine Railway wharf, where it broke up. The wooden vessel was valued at $20,000 and was declared a total loss. Other Rockland ships that were damaged included the bark *Will W. Case*, General Tillson's sloop *Island Belle* and the schooner *Mansfield*.

CITY OF PORTLAND, MAY 8, 1884

Note: City of Portland *should not be confused with the liner* Portland *described in the 1898 gale.*

There were seventy passengers on board the steamer *City of Portland* when it ran on a shoal off Owls Head in the early morning hours. The one-thousand-ton vessel had left Portland and was heading for St. John, New Brunswick, when threatening weather caused the pilot, J.A. Wheeler, to alter course and take the Muscle Ridge Channel. Wheeler did not inform the ship's captain, who had retired to his cabin, nor did he slow the ship as it sped through the narrow channel. The result was that *City of Portland*, running at twelve knows, crashed hard onto Grindstone Ledge. (In Wheeler's defense, it should be noted that a buoy marking the rocks was fifty feet out of position.)

A boat was sent to the mainland for help, and within three hours, the steamer *Rockland* arrived at the scene. All the passengers and their luggage were safely transferred and taken to Rockland. In retrospect, it was fortunate that *City of Portland* had driven so high on the rocks. Had it slid off into deep water, the badly damaged vessel would have sunk rapidly, leaving passengers and crew little time to escape. As it was, worsening weather pounded the wreck until it was destroyed. (Reportedly, ship's artifacts still remain around the ledge.)

CAROLYN, JANUARY 10, 1912

The 289-foot freighter *Carolyn* was bound for New York from Stockton Springs with a cargo of potatoes and paper when it grounded on a ledge off Metinic Island. The *Rockland Opinion* reported that tugs from Rockland and the Coast Guard station at White Head went to the rescue of the steamer stranded in the southwest corner of Penobscot Bay and succeeded in saving the crew. Wreckers then stripped the stricken ship of everything salvageable, and it was given up for lost. *Carolyn*, however, defied the odds. Several months later, a salvage company refloated the vessel. It was towed to Boston, refitted and put back into service. Four years later, *Carolyn* was carrying supplies to Russia during World War I when it ran around off the Kola Peninsula near the city of Murmansk. This time, the ship was not recovered.

CUMBERLAND, MARCH 17, 1917

The tug *Cumberland* met with disaster near the entrance to Carvers Harbor on Vinalhaven while towing a barge carrying nine hundred tons of paving stones. The eighty-seven-foot vessel was piloted by Captain Ralph Curtis and was owned by the Snow Marine Company in Rockland. As described in the *Rockland Opinion*, "When the tug was clearing the harbor, the tow cable became entangled with its propeller placing the craft at the mercy of a northeast gale." *Cumberland* was driven so close to nearby Green Island that Captain Curtis and three crewmembers were able to jump ashore on the rocks. The heavily loaded barge dropped both anchors but had no chance to swing free and soon was also being pounded on the rocks. The wooden *Cumberland*, exposed to the full fury of the storm, was quickly battered to pieces. The steel barge proved more resilient. Although badly damaged by the storm, it was later pulled off when lightened of its load of paving stones. The barge's crewmen also managed to reach Green Island safely, and local fishermen took them all to Vinalhaven. *Cumberland* was valued at $5,000 and was not insured.

EMMA, CIRCA 1930

Another towing catastrophe occurred on a windy winter afternoon when a trawler was towing the sixty-seven-foot schooner *Emma* across Penobscot Bay from Vinalhaven to Rockland. There were two men on board each craft when bad weather drove both vessels out of the channel and onto the Inner Bay Ledges, four miles from the town of Vinalhaven. The four men managed to launch a dory in the freezing weather. They rowed to Vinalhaven against a stiff wind, where Captain Greenlaw called the Coast Guard station at White Head. Unfortunately, the Coast Guard misunderstood the distress call and went to Outer Bay Ledge, seven miles from the wreck. When the men returned to the scene of the double disaster, both vessels were completely lost. Captain Greenlaw had no insurance for *Emma*, which he had purchased four years previously to haul coal and lumber along the coast.

LUTHER LITTLE AND HESPER, 1932

South of Penobscot Bay, at Wiscasset, the schooners *Luther Little* and *Hesper* were probably the two most visible shipwrecks on the Maine coast during the twentieth century.

Luther Little was built in 1917 and plied coastal routes until, following a lengthy grounding, it was brought to Wiscasset by Frank Winter in 1932 to haul coal to interior Maine. *Hesper* was plagued with difficulties beginning with its launching, during which the ways collapsed beneath the ship's weight. *Hesper*

Luther Little and *Hesper* were two wrecked ships that could be seen on the banks of the Sheepscot River at Wiscasset for much of the twentieth century. *Courtesy of Larry Hopkins.*

was also purchased by Frank Winter in 1932 and towed to Wiscasset to join *Luther Little* to haul coal and lumber. Unfortunately, Mr. Winter died shortly afterward. The neglected schooners remained tourist attractions at Wiscasset for many years. Their rotting hulks sat in the mud on the banks of the Sheepscot River long after they became eyesores. They were finally demolished in 1998.

CASTINE, JUNE 8, 1935

On a foggy Saturday morning, the excursion steamer *Castine* cautiously steered its way from across Penobscot Bay toward Vinalhaven. The ship was carrying seventy-five passengers, many of whom were headed for a Grange

The excursion steamer *Castine* sank off the western shores of Vinalhaven on June 8, 1935. *Courtesy of Vinalhaven Historical Society.*

picnic on the island. Four miles from Carvers Harbor, the vessel struck the Inner Bay Ledge, throwing several people into the water. *Castine*'s Captain Leighton Coombs immediately sounded distress signals, which alerted fishing boats in the area, although in the dense fog, it was difficult to locate the stricken vessel. When the steamer *North Haven* finally arrived, it began to take passengers off *Castine*. Seventy-one people were eventually rescued, although sadly, four people died in Vinalhaven's worst marine accident. Today, part of *Castine*'s hull can still be seen on Cedar Island, where it was used as a guesthouse for many years.

AMARETTO, JULY 21, 1985

A fishing vessel with the tasty-sounding name of *Amaretto* was a seventy-one-foot sardine carrier owned by Spencer and Dale Fuller from Rockland. The owners used their boat to transport herring from Vinalhaven to Rockland, where the fish were sold for bait. *Amaretto* served its owners faithfully until, on July 21, 1985, it was stolen from its Rockland berth at the north end of the harbor. When the thieves were discovered fleeing with the vessel, it was scuttled off Monroe Island near Owls Head.

The Fullers offered a $5,000 reward for information leading to the conviction of those who stole their ship. Two months later, the *Bangor Daily News* ran an article stating that a diver from Camden had discovered the probable wreck site on the ocean floor near where debris from *Amaretto* had been seen by the Coast Guard. Apparently, the insurance company was confident enough that the wreck was there that it didn't send down a diver. The Coast Guard has no record as to whether the thieves were ever caught.

HARKNESS, JANUARY 16, 1992

For most of its twenty-eight years, *Harkness* was a heavy-duty tug operated by the Great Northern Paper Company on the Great Lakes until it was purchased by the State of Maine for use as a patrol and research vessel.

On a bitterly cold night, the seventy-five-foot craft was plodding through heavy swells heading for Northeast Harbor. As it crossed Penobscot Bay, helmsman Rudi Musetti realized that *Harkness* was leaking badly. Worse yet, a six-hundred-foot towline had washed overboard, fouling the ship's propeller. When the pumps began to freeze, and with water rising in the engine room, Musetti radioed Rockland for help, and a Coast Guard cutter was immediately dispatched. On Vinalhaven, Dave Allen heard Musetti's call on his scanner and radioed him to head for Matinicus Island. Out on Matinicus, fifty-four-year-old Vance Bunker was alerted and set forth in his thirty-six-foot lobster boat, *Jan-Ellen*, with two companions. By now, visibility was practically zero.

Meanwhile, the now helpless *Harkness* was sinking. The three crewmen donned threadbare immersion suits, and Musetti gave a final fix to the Coast Guard before the tug went down. As the rescue vessels converged on the area, they estimated that *Harkness* had sunk about a mile and a half north of Matinicus near Zephyr Rock. When the two boats spotted each other, they slowly cruised the area for fear of running over bodies.

The three men from *Harkness* were finally spotted clinging to a piece of wreckage (a flashlight had frozen to crewman Arthur Stevens's glove), and they were hauled aboard *Jan-Ellen* more dead than alive. The survivors were taken to Matinicus, where they thawed out in Vance Bunker's house. The next day, they were flown to the mainland and met by TV and newspaper reporters. In March, the Maine legislature honored the lobstermen from *Jan-Ellen* and the Coast Guard crew for their heroism. (I am indebted to Mel R. Allen for his description of the sinking of *Harkness* in *Yankee* magazine.)

Bibliography

Bachelder, Peter Dow. *Shipwrecks & Maritime Disasters of the Maine Coast.* Portland, ME: Provincial Press, 1997.

Bachelder, Peter Dow, and Mason Philip Smith. *Four Short Blasts: The Gale of 1898 and the Loss of the Steamer Portland.* Portland, ME: Provincial Press, 2003.

Chapelle, Howard I. *The History of American Sailing Ships.* New York: W.W. Norton, 1955.

Chatto, Clarence I., and Clair E. Turner. *Register of the Towns of Sedgwick, Brooklin, Deer Isle, Stonington and Isle au Haut.* Brooklin, ME, 1905.

Conforti, Joseph A. *Creating Portland, History and Place in Northern New England.* Durham: University of New Hampshire Press, 2005.

Daughan, George C. *1812: The Navy's War.* New York: Basic Books, 2011.

———. *If by Sea: The Forging of the American Navy.* New York: Basic Books, 2008.

D'Entremont, Jeremy. *Great Shipwrecks of the Maine Coast.* Beverly, MA: Commonwealth Editions, 2012.

Duncan, Roger F. *Coastal Maine: A Maritime History.* Woodstock, VT: Countryman Press, 1992.

Farrow, John Pendleton. *History of Islesboro, 1893–1983.* Portland, ME: Seavey Printers, 1984.

Gross, Clayton. *Island Chronicles: Accounts of Days Past in Deer Isle and Stonington.* Stonington, ME: Penobscot Bay Press, 1977.

Heckman, Richard, ed. *Yankees Under Sail.* Dublin, NH: Yankee Inc., 1968.

Hosmer, George. *An Historical Sketch of the Town of Deer Isle, Maine*. Boston: Fort Hill Press, 1905.

Islesboro Historical Society. *History of Islesboro, 1764–1892*. Rockland, ME: Picton Press, 1893.

Lapham, William B. *In Memoriam: The Hon. Joseph R. Bodwell*. Augusta, ME: Burleigh & Flint, 1888.

Leamon, James. *Revolution Downeast*. Amherst: University of Massachusetts Press, 1993.

Long, Charles F. *Matinicus Isle*. Lewiston, ME: Lewiston Journal Printshop, 1926.

Morgan, James Morris. *Recollections of a Rebel Reefer*. Boston: Houghton Mifflin, 1917.

Morris, Charles. *The Autobiography of Commodore Charles Morris, USN*. Annapolis, MD: Naval Institute Press, 2002.

Mowat, Henry. *Voyage of the Canceaux*. Annotated by Andrew J. Wahll. Bowie, MD: Heritage Books Inc., 2003.

O'Leary, Wayne M. *Maine Sea Fisheries*. Boston: Northeastern University Press, 1996.

O'Neill, Helen. "Setting the Record Straight: The Sinking of PE-56." *Sea Classics* magazine (2003).

Post, Larkin A. "S.S. *Polias*: A Prototype of the World War I Concrete Ship Program." Master's thesis, East Carolina University, 2007.

Puleo, Stephen. *Due to Enemy Action*. Guilford, CT: Lyons Press, 2005.

Quinn, William P. *Shipwrecks Around Maine*. Orleans, MA: Lower Cape Publishing Company, 1983.

———. *Shipwrecks Around New England*. New Bedford, MA: Reynolds-DeWalt Publishing Company, 1979.

Richardson, John. *Steamboat Lore of the Penobscot*. Augusta, ME: Kennebec Journal Print Shop, 1945.

Rowe, William Hutchinson. *The Maritime History of Maine*. Gardiner, ME: Harpswell Press, 1948.

Snow, Bertram. *The Maine Beam*. Rockland, ME: Lakeside Printing Company, 2005.

Snow, Edward Rowe. *Great Gales and Dire Disasters*. New York: Dodd, Mead & Company, 1952.

———. *Great Storms and Famous Shipwrecks of the New England Coast*. Boston: Yankee Publishing Company, 1946.

———. *New England Sea Tragedies*. New York: Dodd, Mead & Company, 1960.

Swett, Sophie. *Stories of Maine*. New York: American Book Company, 1899.

Symonds, Craig L. *The Civil War at Sea*. New York: Oxford University Press, 2012.

Wasson, George. *Sailing Days on the Penobscot*. Salem, MA: Marine Research Society, 1932.

Williamson, Joseph, and Alfred Johnson. *History of Belfast Maine*. Vol. 2. Belfast, ME: New England History Press, 2010.

ARCHIVAL MATERIAL CONSULTED AT THE FOLLOWING LOCATIONS

Belfast Public Library, Special Collections, Belfast, Maine.

Castine Historical Society, Castine, Maine.

Deer Isle and Stonington Historical Society, Deer Isle, Maine.

Gilder Lehrman Institute of American History, New York City, New York.

Hampden Historical Society, Hampden, Maine.

Islesboro Historical Society, Islesboro, Maine.

Maine Historical Society, Portland, Maine.

Marshall Point Lighthouse Museum, Port Clyde, Maine.

Penobscot Marine Museum Library, Searsport, Maine.

Rockland Historical Society, Rockland, Maine.

Rockland Public Library, Rockland, Maine.

Thomaston Historical Society, Thomaston, Maine.

Vinalhaven Historical Society, Vinalhaven, Maine.

Vinalhaven Public Library, Vinalhaven, Maine.

About the Author

H arry Gratwick is a lifelong summer
resident of Vinalhaven Island in
Penobscot Bay. A retired history teacher,
Gratwick had a forty-six-year career as
a secondary school teacher, coach and
administrator. He spent most of these
years at Germantown Friends School
in Philadelphia, Pennsylvania, where
he chaired the history department and
coached the baseball team.

Harry is an active member of the
Vinalhaven Historical Society and has
written extensively on maritime history
for two Island Institute publications, the
Working Waterfront and the *Island Journal.*
Historic Shipwrecks of Penobscot Bay is his
sixth book about Maine.

Gratwick is a graduate of Williams College and has a master's degree
from Columbia University. Harry and his wife, Tita, spend the winter
months in Philadelphia. They have two grown sons, a Russian daughter-
in-law and two grandsons.

Visit him at www.harrygratwick.com.